The
Criticism
of
Prose

S. H. BURTON

Longman

LONGMAN GROUP LIMITED
London

*Associated companies, branches and representatives
throughout the world*

© Longman Group Limited 1973

First published 1973
Second impression 1975
ISBN 0 582 34107 8

Printed in Hong Kong by
Wing Tai Cheung Printing Co. Ltd.

Contents

Acknowledgements

We are grateful to the following for permission to reproduce copyright material:

Author's agents, Miss Sonia Brownall and Secker & Warburg Ltd for an extract from 'Why I Write' from *Such, Such Were the Joys* by George Orwell; Jonathan Cape Ltd, for an extract from 'Darkness at Noon' by Arthur Koestler; Author's agents for an extract from *A House and its Head* by Ivy Compton-Burnett; André Deutsch Ltd for an extract from *The Mystic Masseur* by V. S. Naipaul; Author for an extract from 'Whither Wigwams' from *Meet My Maker the Mad Molecule* by J. P. Donleavy; Eyre & Spottiswoode Ltd, for an extract from *Riders in the Chariot* by Patrick White; Author for an extract from *Cold Comfort Farm* by Stella Gibbons; Hutchinson Publishing Group Ltd, for an extract from 'Creed of an Architect' by John Killick and 'Thoughts on Running' by Herb Greer from *The Schweppes Book of the New Generation*; Author's agents and the Estate of the Late Mrs Frieda Lawrence for extracts from *Phoenix* and *The White Peacock* by D. H. Lawrence; The Hogarth Press Ltd, for an extract from *A Rose for Winter* by Laurie Lee; Longman Group Ltd, for an extract from 'Number Nine Rock' by John Braine; from *New Statesmanship* ed. by Edward Hyams; Macmillan & Co Ltd, Basingstoke, and The Macmillan Company of Canada Ltd for an extract from *Far from the Madding Crowd* by Thomas Hardy; *New Statesman* for an extract from 'Women in Adversity' by Keith Thomas, a major review of *The Captive Wife* by Hannah Gavron from *New Statesman* May 66; Oliver & Boyd for an extract from *Ezra Pound* by G. S. Fraser; Oxford University Press for an extract from *Splendid Fairing* by Constance Holme; Penguin Books Ltd, for an extract from *The Modern Writer and His World* by G. S. Fraser; Sidgwick & Jackson Ltd, for an extract from 'Democracy and the Arts' from *The Prose of Rupert Brooke* edited by Christopher Hassall and Author and Author's agents for an extract from *Saturday Night and Sunday Morning* by Alan Sillitoe.

Preface

The aim of this book is to suggest and to illustrate useful approaches to criticism. Attention is drawn to overall structure and to the arrangement and presentation of argument. Diction, imagery, and rhythm are then examined. At each stage of the developing exposition, examples are worked and passages for practice are provided. This practice material varies greatly in length to permit either intensive examination of short passages or sustained study of longer extracts. A great variety of prose, both historical and contemporary, is represented, and Section II consists entirely of modern passages for comprehension and criticism.

I have given considerable space to prose rhythms—a topic more often mentioned than discussed in detail—and I acknowledge with gratitude help received on this subject from Paull Franklin Baum's *The Other Harmony of Prose* (Duke University Press, 1952).

Finally, I must stress that *The Criticism of Prose* makes no attempt to lay down rules; but the starting points provided here have been found useful by my pupils, and I am, therefore, encouraged to think that they may prove helpful to others in evolving their own critical methods.

S. H. BURTON

1
Introduction

Prose is often found harder to criticise than poetry. There are several reasons for this. First, there is the apparent formlessness of prose as compared with poetry. In poetry, metre and stanza form make an immediate impact on the reader. They are seen at once as two of the means by which the poet is trying to achieve his chosen ends (Even in free verse, an immediately perceptible rhythm attracts the reader's attention.) But a prose passage seems shapeless. Important as structure and rhythm are in prose, few readers have ears and eyes trained to recognise their effects.

The second reason is related to the first. In 'practical criticism' the reader is often faced with a complete poem, or at least a self-contained selection of verses; but the prose passage for criticism is almost always–and obviously–an extract. This makes it harder to appreciate its shape and so adds to the difficulty of seeing the prose writer's means in relation to his ends.

Again, too many readers adopt a rigid attitude. They assume that they know what 'good prose' *ought* to be. But the infinite variety of prose cannot be confined in such a straitjacket. A good critic distrusts general rules about 'good' and 'bad' prose. Writing that is well adapted to a writer's purpose is good: writing that is not well adapted to a writer's purposes is bad. (In his final judgment of a piece of writing the critic may conclude that, though it was well done, it was not worth doing–but that is a different matter.)

It follows that the critic's first job is to understand what the writer is saying and to discover his purpose in saying it. That done, he can begin to explore the effectiveness of the writer's use of language.

2

Sense, tone, and intention

It is impossible to reach a fair judgment of any piece of writing without considering it first under these three headings.

I SENSE

This is the literal meaning of the passage. This must be established first, for criticism without comprehension is impossible. Careful reading is necessary, the critic keeping his mind open and working with the writer. Worry about what the writer is saying, not about what you think he ought to be saying. This essential first step to criticism will often entail close inspection of the relationship between sentence and sentence *and* between paragraph and paragraph. To follow the developing presentation of argument, exposition, or emotion requires sustained and sympathetic attention on the critic's part.

II TONE

This reflects the writer's attitude to his subject and to his readers. Many different kinds of verbal signals may be employed to communicate this attitude: word order; turns of phrase; choice of words; sentence structure; literary or historical allusions or quotations. Nobody can list all the resources open to a skilled writer. The critic has to look out for and listen to the visual and aural signals, asking himself as he recognises each one: 'What does that tell me about what this writer is feeling and about what he is trying to do?'

III INTENTION

This is the purpose underlying the writing. Again, no list can enumerate all the possibilities: the writer may be trying to communicate information, to arouse feeling, to form opinions. He may be trying to do all or some of these things at once. The critic must become aware of what is being attempted and, in relation to the each passage that he reads, he must refine his description of intention from a broad category into an accurate particularisation. Grasp of meaning and sensitiveness to tone are, of course, crucial to success in discerning intention.

FOR PRACTICE

1

Today science has become an important way of thought. Indeed, it is probably the most important intellectual influence in our modern philosophy. There is a danger, therefore, that it may tend to be taken too solemnly, too uncritically. We consider science to be the precise assessment and collation of facts. Any conclusions drawn from these facts must be verifiable by experiment. But one thing that has been unduly neglected by scientists is the old question as to whether a tree that falls in the desert makes any noise when nobody is there to hear it. And this is odd because it was Einstein, the greatest of them all, who pointed out that any particular scientist was mistaken in assuming that two things happened simultaneously in two different places when he could never be in two places at once to see both things occurring. Einstein, in fact, pointed out in his polite mathematics, which were mercifully incomprehensible not only to lay people but to most scientists as well, that confident scientific assumptions—for example, that two separate events happen simultaneously—might be humbug. Quite recently, however, there is some evidence that the tide of scientific solemnity is turning. One or two papers have appeared in the literature that discuss humbug seriously. And it may not be long before it is recognised that humbug plays an important role in certain branches of science.

MAGNUS PYKE *Humbug in Science*

1 Briefly summarise the argument of that passage.

2 Give your reasons – drawn from the passage itself – for thinking that the writer is or is not serious, quoting particular words and phrases that seem to signal tone.

3 What, in the light of your answers to questions 1 and 2, do you take to be the writer's purpose?

2

I think that is an admirably humane document, in its expression a model of professional lucidity without jargon. And I am very glad, for Pound's sake, that the Medical Board arrived at this decision; if he had been put on trial, it would have been impossible to acquit and politically very difficult to pardon him. I have seen transcripts only of a very few of his broadcasts, mainly on literary subjects; I have been told that others contained virulently anti-Semitic propaganda. Pound no doubt thought very sincerely that, in giving them, he was defending America, or what America should be. But, of course, whatever the content had been, making the broadcasts at all laid him open to an indictment for treason; America was at war with Italy, he was, by broadcasting from an Italian station, giving aid and comfort to the enemy, and that was that. The decision of the Medical Board saved him from life imprisonment, perhaps from death.

At the same time, some of the remarks in the report make me wonder just how sane, by the verdict of a committee of psychiatrists, any poet is. I have known a great many poets in my time. A great majority of them 'make an uncertain living by writing poetry and criticism'; good poets often do tend to be 'grandiose, expansive and exuberant in manner'; they can also often be recognised (especially when one of their books has been reviewed unfavourably, or a rival poet is getting too much publicity) as 'eccentric, querulous, and egocentric'. They quite often do have some obsessional interest, that seems at first sight to have little to do with poetry, like Pound's economics. Perhaps all poets *are* a little mad: one talks of 'mad poets' as one talks of 'mad majors'.

The creative process puts a continuing strain on the whole organism, on the intelligence and sensibility, and in a way also it isolates the creative person, in a way that the uncreative (however full of intelligence and good will) may find it hard to understand.

G. S. FRASER Ezra Pound

1 What was the Medical Board's decision? Quote evidence from the passage in support of your answer.
2 Briefly summarise the argument of the passage, bringing out the differing emphases of the two paragraphs.
3 What changes of tone can you detect in the second paragraph?
4 What conclusions can be drawn from this passage about the writer's own opinions on life and literature?

3

What purposes have the writers of the following two passages in common? Which passage do you prefer, and why? Quote briefly from the passages in support of your answer to each question.

[A]

It swelled his little throat and gushed from him with thrilling force and plenty, and every time he checked his song to think of its theme, the green meadows, the quiet stealing streams, the clover he first soared from and Spring he sang so well, a loud sigh from many a rough bosom, many a wild and wicked heart, told how tight the listeners had held their breath to hear him; and when he swelled with song again, and poured with all his soul the green meadows, the quiet brooks, the honey clover, and the English Spring, the rugged mouths opened and so stayed, and the shaggy lips trembled, and more than one drop trickled from fierce unbridled hearts down bronzed and rugged cheeks. *Dulce domum!*

And these shaggy men, full of oaths and strife and cupidity, had once been little white-headed boys, and had strolled about the English fields with little sisters and little brothers, and seen the lark rise, and heard him sing this very song. The little playmates lay in the churchyard, and they were full of oaths and drink and lusts and remorses, but no note was changed in this immortal song. And so for a moment or two years of vice rolled away like a dark cloud from the memory, and the past shone out in the song-shine; they came back, bright as the immortal notes that lighted them, those faded pictures and those fleeted days; the cottage, the old mother's tears when he left her without one grain of sorrow; the village church and its simple chimes; the clover field hard by in which he lay and gambolled, while the lark praised God over-head, the chubby playmates that never grew to be wicked, the sweet hours of youth, and innocence, and home!

CHARLES READE *It's Never too Late to Mend*

[B]

They buried him in the cathedral which he had loved so well, and in which nearly all the work of his life had been done; and all Barchester was there to see him laid in his grave within the cloisters. There was no procession of coaches, no hearse, nor was there any attempt at funereal pomp. From the dean's side-door, across the vaulted passage, and into the transept— over the little step upon which he had so nearly fallen when last he made his way out of the building–the coffin was carried on men's shoulders. It was but a short journey from his bedroom to his grave. But the bell had been tolling sadly all the morning, and the nave and the aisles and the transepts, close up to the door leading from the transept into the cloister, were crowded with those who had known the name and the figure and the voice of Mr Harding as long as they had known anything. Up to this day no one would have said specially that Mr Harding was a favourite in the town. He had never been forward enough in anything to become the acknowledged possessor of popularity. But, now he was gone, men and women told each other how good he had been. They remembered the sweetness of his smile, and talked of loving little words which he had spoken to them–either years ago or the other day, for his words had always been loving.

ANTHONY TROLLOPE *The Last Chronicle of Barset*

3
What kind of writing is this?

Section 2 emphasised that the critic must understand the writer's intentions before he can judge his success or failure, for we can meaningfully fault a piece of writing only if we can show that it is not well adapted to its author's purposes. Certain broad categories of intention–to arouse emotion, to present facts, to persuade through argument–were given as illustrations of different purposes in writing; but it was stressed that the critic must refine such broad classifications into more precise descriptions before he can claim to appreciate a particular writer's intention in a particular passage.

The writer, however, does not often state explicitly what his purposes are. The reader must usually deduce intention from the content and tone, responding as sensitively as possible to the language used. Before he attempts to judge a piece of writing, the critic must answer the question, *What kind of writing is this*? and then judge solely within the terms of reference supplied by the answer to that question. If the passage is technical, then different linguistic features will be appropriate compared with those marking a passage of creative writing. A political party press release will show different features of grammar and vocabulary from those that characterise a scientific dissertation on the migratory routes of swallows; and the latter will involve a choice of linguistic resources different from that appropriate to a critical essay on the *Odes* of John Keats.

The following headings will be found useful when answering the question 'What kind of writing is this?' Not all the tests proposed are relevant in every case but, with practice, the critic will learn to recognise which tests can be usefully applied to any given passage. Methodical application in the early stages will lead to a more rapid–'instinctive'–way of working. The critical insight developed by a proficient judge grows out of a planned approach based on sound principles.

I SENSE

What is this passage about? It is not safe to assume that the passage means what it seems to mean at first reading. (See Section 7 for a discussion of direct and indirect expression.)

II TONE

What is the writer's attitude to his material and to his readers? Is he serious or flippant?–grave or gay?–satirical or approving?–ironical or 'straight'? (The possibilities cannot be exhausted in a list: reading background and critical practice will extend the critic's range and refine his analysis.) What linguistic features are used to signal the dominant tone of the passage and to signal changes of tone within it?

III GENRE

What literary classification can be applied to the passage? Is it taken from a novel? If so, what kind of a novel–psychological, social, satirical, etc.? Does it come from an essay? If so, what kind of an essay–autobiographical, literary, discursive, etc.? Is it historical writing?–scientific?–political? These are, of course, only a few of the possibilities.

IV HISTORICAL PERIOD

A living language changes a great deal with the passage of time. Consequently, the linguistic resources available to a writer and the conventions appropriate to a particular literary genre will vary from period to period. For example, a passage taken from the work of an eighteenth-century novelist will differ linguistically and conventionally from a text taken from the work of a twentieth-century novelist. The critic must allow for this in forming his judgments, for the novel-writing conventions open to, say, James Joyce (and expanded by him) were not those within which, say, Henry Fielding was operating; and the linguistic resources available to Sir Walter Scott were very different from those now in general use. Then, too, the critic must allow for shifts in word meaning and for historical changes in idiom and grammar.

V VARIETIES OF LANGUAGE

Writers–and creative writers in particular–may choose to employ, either in the whole passage or in parts of it, some non-standard variety of the language–slang, dialect, technical terms, etc. Any such variation from standard English must be noted by the critic. It may be a pointer to the writer's particular purposes, and its effect, therefore, important in forming a critical judgment.

VI SPOKEN OR WRITTEN DISCOURSE

Although we are concerned here with the written word, it is important to remember that writers often imitate speech. To take the extreme example first, a verbatim report of a conversation or of a speech will exhibit characteristics appropriate to the spoken– but inappropriate to the written–word. The critic who fails to recognise the 'mode of language' being employed will go astray in his judgment by applying the wrong criteria. Again, in dealing with creative writing–particularly with passages taken from novels or plays–he must watch for signals indicating that the writer wants what he *writes* to be read as if it were *spoken*. This is not simply a matter of employing such graphological devices as quotation marks. The novelist may choose to represent a character's thoughts in 'interior monologue' or in direct monologue. He may choose to represent speech, not directly, but as if it were being 'overheard' by the reader or by another character. Such speech may come out not as if being said by one character but as if being heard by another. Such variations between spoken and written language may play a very important part in literature–in the novels of Dickens, for example–and they are, therefore, of great importance to the critic.

VII FORMALITY OR INFORMALITY

The degree of formality in the writing is largely a question of writer/reader relationship. The formality appropriate to a scientific textbook is not appropriate to a volume of essays in which the writer's standpoint is personal and subjective. A novelist or a dramatist will often convey characterisation or shifts in relationship between characters by employing varying degrees of formality. Different historical periods and different purposes or literary conventions may be reflected in strikingly different

9

degrees of formality in the presentation or mode of narration of novels.

Rude travel is enticing to us English. And so are its records; even though the adventurer be no pilgrim of love. And antique friendship has at least the interest of a fossil. *Still, as the true centre of this story is in Holland, it is full time to return thither*, and to those ordinary personages and incidents whereof life has been mainly composed in all ages.

CHARLES READE *The Cloister and the Hearth*

As that extract shows, the narrative devices of a Victorian novelist may seem stiff and artificial when compared with those of many twentieth-century novelists, who adopt an extreme informality, not only in their writing of dialogue – where the relationship of character with character is brought out – but also in those passages in which the desired relationship of novelist to reader is indicated.

Obviously, all the above elements interact. The sense, the tone, the use of written or 'spoken' language and the degree of formality in the writing are interrelated: the genre and the historical period affect and are affected by the other features.

Some useful categories into which the various kinds of prose may be divided are: 1. Argumentative; 2. Critical; 3. Descriptive; 4. Dramatic; 5. Expository; 6. Narrative; 7. Oratorical; 8. Philosophical; 9. Satirical.

A text may, of course, combine several of those functions. Shifts from one to another within a passage should be noted.

From careful attempts to identify the kind of writing represented by the passage under consideration, the critic may expect two main results:

Firstly, those features of the passage that struck with most force at first reading will now be seen more clearly in relation to the text *as a whole*. This provides a useful check on the validity of first impressions. Secondly, uses of language that were overlooked at first reading will be brought out, and their importance relative to the more obvious features of the writing will be suggested.

Asking the question, 'What kind of writing is this?' initiates a search for the linguistic features in the writing that correspond to the first responses that the critic has made to the text. When he comes to examine the diction, imagery, and rhythms he will continue the search so begun, looking always for uses of language that support and clarify his responses *and modify or reject those responses for which he is unable to find adequate text support.*

It is only through such text-based investigation that the critic can hope to proceed to an informed and imaginative final judgment.

FOR PRACTICE

1
Apply to each of the following passages the tests just described, in order to answer the question, 'What kind of writing is this?' Then judge each passage as a successful or unsuccessful piece of writing. Use evidence from each passage in support of your judgment.

[A]
And when matins and the first mass was done, there was seen in the churchyard against the high altar a great stone four square, like unto a marble stone, and in the midst thereof was like an anvil of steel a foot on high, and therein stack a fair sword naked by the point, and letters there were written in gold about the sword that said thus: Whoso pulleth out this sword of this stone and anvil is rightwise king born of all England.

SIR THOMAS MALORY Le Morte d'Arthur

[B]
SWORD A weapon adapted for cutting and thrusting, consisting of a handle or *hilt* with a cross-guard, and a straight or curved blade with either one or two sharp edges (or sometimes with blunt edges) and a sharp point. *fig.* Something that wounds or kills, a cause of death or destruction, a destroying agency; also something figured as a weapon of attack in spiritual warfare.

[C]
A 14th century Japanese sword
The blade is of hon-zukuri form with a wide full-length groove in each shinogi; the back is futsumune, the jagane

rather wide with funbari and the curvature is medium torii-zori; the tempering is notare midare, becoming gonome towards the point, with dense nie in the haman and many sunagashi or 'drifting sand' formations.

> From a saleroom catalogue, as quoted by *The Times*.

2

Apply the 'what-kind-of-writing?' tests to these passages, commenting on the similarities and differences between them that such an examination reveals.

[A]

'So the children are not down yet?' said Ellen Edgeworth. Her husband gave her a glance, and turned his eyes towards the window.

'So the children are not down yet?' she said on a note of question.

Mr Edgeworth put his finger down his collar and settled his neck.

'So you are down first, Duncan?' said his wife, as though putting her observation in a more acceptable form.

Duncan returned his hand to his collar with a frown.

Duncan Edgeworth was a man of medium height and build, appearing both to others and to himself to be tall. He had narrow, grey eyes, stiff, grey hair and beard, a solid, aquiline face, young for his sixty-six years, and a stiff, imperious bearing. His wife was a small, spare, sallow woman, a few years younger, with large, kind, prominent eyes, a long, thin, questioning nose, and a harried, innocent, somehow fulfilled expression.

The day was Christmas Day in the year eighteen eighty-five, and the room was the usual dining-room of an eighteenth-century country house. The later additions to the room had honourable place, and every opportunity to dominate its character, and used the last in the powerful manner of objects of the Victorian age, seeming in so doing to rank themselves with their possessor.

'So you are down first of all, Duncan,' said Ellen, employing a note of propitiation, as if it would serve its purpose.

Her husband implied by lifting his shoulders that he could hardly deny it.

'The children are late, are they not?' said Ellen, to whom speech clearly ranked above silence.

Duncan indicated by the same movement that his attitude was the same.

'I think there are more presents than usual. Oh, I wish they would all come down.'

'Why do you wish it?'

'Well, it is not a day when we want them to be late, is it?'

'Do we want them to be late on any day? Oh, of course, it is Christmas Day. I saw the things on the table.'

Ellen also saw them.

'Oh, you have been down first, and put your presents at the places!'

Duncan moved his neck with an air of satisfaction in the ease he had attained.

'I think they will all be down soon,' said his wife, her manner seeming to carry comfort.

'Will they?' just uttered her husband, looking at the wall as if something on it struck him.

'They won't be very late on Christmas Day.'

'Why should they be late on Christmas Day or any other? What reason would you suppose?'

Ellen did not say.

IVY COMPTON-BURNETT *A House and Its Head*

[B]

He turned in at the yard-end. Dusk was spreading between the houses, turning into a cold, windy April evening. His heavy boots clobbered their way down the yard. Lifting the backdoor latch he passed through the scullery and hung his coat in the parlour. He usually said: 'Hey-up', to the rest of the family, but this evening he was too preoccupied for

13

politeness, seating himself morosely at the table and waiting for his mother to pour him a cup of tea. The wireless was drumming away, and the first thing he said was:

'Turn that thing off.'

But it was playing some Old Time waltzes that his mother liked. 'Leave it on,' she said, 'It's nice music.'

'Well, pour me a cup o' tea, then,' he demanded.

She looked up at him. 'What's up wi' yo' tonight? Pullin' a megrim like that.'

He didn't answer. The wireless was left on. His elder brother Fred sat at the table doing a crossword. He wondered what was on Arthur's mind, seeing him drink his tea without saying a word. 'I'm going upstairs to listen to the wireless,' Fred announced.

Arthur followed him, and sat on the bed.

'You don't seem very happy,' Fred said. 'What's the trouble?'

He didn't want to explain his worries. 'Nowt,' he answered in the last stages of dejection. Lighting a cigarette he walked to the window and hurled the dead match outside as if it were a stone and he wanted to hit someone; stood for a moment to watch kids playing beneath the lighted street-lamps, hearing the distant hooting of factory engines at the end of the terrace. 'If you want to know what's up,' he said, 'two blokes are after me, a couple of swaddies'–and he told everything. 'Winnie's husband's on leave from Germany, and he's out with one of his pals to get me before they go back.'

'Keep out of their way for a bit, then,' Fred advised him. 'Are you going out tonight?'

'I was thinking about it.'

'I'll go with you. I'd like a walk.' If I can't help him much in a fight I can at least see that he doesn't get into one, Fred told himself.

'Are you sure you want to come?' He didn't feel like leading Fred into any trouble. With himself, it didn't matter.

'I said I wanted a walk, didn't I?'

'It's your funeral then,' Arthur warned him.

'And yours,' Fred retorted, 'for getting mixed-up in a thing like this.'

Neither used overcoats, hoping to warm themselves by a quick walk to the pub, and then to be re-stoked by a pint or two. Fred admitted, walking up the yard, that he was broke as usual–thirty-bob sickness benefit didn't go far–and Arthur said that the drinks would be on him. Mrs Bull stood at the yard-end, her moon-face a beacon scanning the street for news of established wrecks and for rumours of those next destined for the dogs, peering through half-darkness to find out who was nipping to Taylor's for a basket of grub on tick. Arthur unknowingly nudged her in passing.

'Mind what yer doin',' she shouted after him. 'Yer young bleeder.'

ALAN SILLITOE *Saturday Night and Sunday Morning*

[C]

'Olive will come down in about ten minutes; she told me to tell you that. About ten; that is exactly like Olive. Neither five nor fifteen, and yet not ten exactly, but either nine or eleven. She didn't tell me to say she was glad to see you, because she doesn't know whether she is or not, and she wouldn't for the world expose herself to telling a fib. She is very honest, is Olive Chancellor; she is full of rectitude. Nobody tells fibs in Boston; I don't know what to make of them all. Well, I am very glad to see you, at any rate.'

These words were spoken with much volubility by a fair, plump, smiling woman who entered a narrow drawing-room in which a visitor, kept waiting a few moments, was already absorbed in a book. The gentleman had not even needed to sit down to become interested: apparently he had taken up the volume from a table as soon as he came in, and, standing there, after a single glance round the apartment, had lost himself in its pages. He threw it down at the approach of Mrs Luna, laughed, shook hands with her, and said in answer to her last remark, 'You imply that you do tell fibs. Perhaps that is one.'

15

'Oh no; there is nothing wonderful in my being glad to see you, 'Mrs Luna rejoined, 'when I tell you that I have been three long weeks in this unprevaricating city.'

'That has an unflattering sound for me,' said the young man. 'I pretend not to prevaricate.'

'Dear me, what's the good of being a Southerner?' the lady asked. 'Olive told me to tell you she hoped you will stay to dinner. And if she said it, she really does hope it. She is willing to risk that.'

'Just as I am?' the visitor inquired, presenting himself with rather a work-a-day aspect.

Mrs Luna glanced at him from head to foot, and gave a little smiling sigh, as if he had been a long sum in addition. And, indeed, he was very long, Basil Ransom, and he even looked a little hard and discouraging, like a column of figures, in spite of the friendly face which he bent upon his hostess's deputy, and which, in its thinness, had a deep dry line, a sort of premature wrinkle, on either side of the mouth. He was tall and lean, and dressed throughout in black; his shirt-collar was low and wide, and the triangle of linen, a little crumpled, exhibited by the opening of his waistcoat, was adorned by a pin containing a small red stone. In spite of this decoration the young man looked poor—as poor as a young man could look who had a fine head and such magnificent eyes.

HENRY JAMES *The Bostonians*

3

Basing your answer on your close examination of those three passages, and referring to the evidence supplied by each, attempt a definition of the novel.

4
Style: its function and its elements

Once the critic is sure that he understands the sense of the passage, that he has tuned in accurately to its tone, that he has grasped the writer's purposes and identified the kind of writing, he can go on to the next stage of his work: namely, to assess the effectiveness of the linguistic means employed by the writer. This assessment is sometimes called the judgment of style, and that description will do–provided that we are clear that 'style' is a blend of various elements; and clear, too, that there is no such thing as 'good' or 'bad' style in the abstract. Good style–good writing–is a use of language which advances the writer's purposes. Bad style–bad writing–is that which impedes the writer's purposes.

The chief elements of style are: diction, imagery, and rhythm. Each is now discussed in a separate section of this book. But it is not thereby suggested that there is one infallible scheme of criticism that all readers should adopt. The critical process is complex and highly individual. Critical methods will rightly vary from reader to reader. Indeed, each individual reader-critic will vary his own critical methods as his sensitiveness and experience guide him to select the critical tools appropriate to the particular passage that confronts him. The suggestions made here should be seen *as* suggestions, designed to provide useful starting points from which individual methods may be evolved.

5
The critical sequence

The first reading of a passage may make a strong impression, favourable or unfavourable, upon the reader. That first impression may or may not persist throughout the successive stages of the critical process and may or may not form the basis of his final judgment, for each successive stage of the evolving criticism is a text-based check on first impressions, in the course of which the initial reactions may be considerably modified. The critical sequence may be conveniently divided into these stages: I Reception; II Analysis; III Final judgment.

I RECEPTION
The first reading is the stage during which the reader tries to receive and respond to the text as a whole, when 'meaning' and 'style'★ – matter and manner – *together* operate upon his intelligence and his sensitivity to produce the initial impact. At this stage a good reader opens his mind as fully as possible to the writer, responsive to him as far as lies in his power and receptive to the text as a whole. But though such a first reading is the essential preliminary to good judgment, the critic has a lot more work to do. First impressions are notoriously unreliable. Different readers may react in very different ways at a first reading who will yet, after careful re-consideration, agree about a text over which they were at first in dispute.

II ANALYSIS
The analytical stage of the critical sequence begins with the understanding of the sense, the recognition of tone and intention,

★The two terms are quoted because it is impossible to separate the two elements: *how* something is said affects *what* is said; *what* is said influences *how* it is said.

and the identification of the kind of writing. Analysis continues as the stylistic methods (choice of words or diction, imagery, and rhythm) are examined and judged in the light of the writer's purposes.

III FINAL JUDGMENT

In his final judgment the critic takes into account both his objective analysis and his subjective responses. Criticism, in other words, is an art, not a science. The sympathetic reading of a text, followed by detailed, analytical scrutiny, will achieve as high a degree of objectivity as is possible in the critical art. But the final judgment arises out of the interplay of two minds—the writer's and the critic's. Valuable descriptive criticism* is necessarily based on such an interplay. The writer is entitled to expect careful, unprejudiced and sympathetic reading; but the good critic has a mind of his own, and his final opinion is as much a self-judgment (and a self-revelation) as it is a judgment of the writer.

The successive stages of the critical sequence are not, of course, neatly blocked off from each other. An ordered procedure is essential, but the results thrown up by each stage flow into and influence the other stages. The critical sequence develops spirally, not in a straight line. Reception cannot be insulated from analysis, nor the subjective elements from the objective. For instance, a first impression of a text may be that the writing is 'picturesque'. Throughout the analytical stage the critic will be looking for the linguistic features that support that first impression. In so doing, he may confirm, reject, or modify the 'label' that he first attached to the text. Thus the subjective nature of the first critical stage gives direction to the analysis; and the analysis itself refers back to—monitors and is monitored by—the reception. Equally, the last stage, the final judgment, blends the objective and the subjective, referring to and springing out of the analysis and at the same time voicing the critic's own opinion of the overall purposes and achievement of the writer.

An 'absolute' objectivity is neither possible nor desirable. The critic must in the end come out with *his* opinion: an opinion tested

*Descriptive criticism: 'the analysis of existing literary works' (George Watson: *The Literary Critics*); so called to distinguish it from legislative criticism and theoretical criticism. 'Practical criticism'—a term much used today—may be defined as the descriptive criticism of extracts from existing literary works.

and tempered by the close scrutiny–the 'objective' assessments–
of the analytical stage; but an opinion that is the product of the
intellect, imagination, taste and experience of the individual
critic.

FOR PRACTICE

Make an analysis of each of the following passages under these
headings: 1. Sense or subject matter; 2. Tone; 3. Writer's intention; 4. Kind of writing (the categories suggested in Section 3 may
be useful). Briefly summarise the argument of the starred passages.

[A]

The Old Vicarage was a long, ramshackle, three-storeyed
house of red brick, with attics and dormer windows in a high
roof; at the back was a veranda, sagging in places, and
canopied all along with virginia creeper, and a profuse,
overgrown, sweet-smelling garden with random trees,
mostly ancient chestnuts, enclosing the demesne; a lawn
ending in long grass, giant trees, and briars on the river bank
where the water flowed four feet deep; and here and there
stray relics of the nineteenth century–on the lawn a cement
sundial in the form of a book lying open on a lectern, a
cement basin with a fountain in the centre, and the sham
Gothic ruin in a far corner, overhung with branches; and to
one side stood Mr Neeve's orderly beehives, concealed among
the thickets. A five-barred gate, always hooked back among
the bushes, stood at one corner of the gravelled approach,
giving access from the road; the whole property was shut in
by trees entangled with ivy, and the nearness of the river
filled the air with the smell of dampness. Brooke rented
three rooms; at the top of his part of the stairs there was a low
wicket gate, for his bedroom had been a nursery, and he
would tell how on going up late at night it was almost as if
the ghosts of Victorian children plucked at his sleeve;
beneath it was the living-room, a round table in the centre
littered with books and letters, and a glass door with yellow
panes of *art nouveau* design which, he said, gave him the

illusion of sunshine on a wet day, shadowed by strands of creeper from the veranda roof beyond, led out on to the lawn. The branches of an old box-tree also darkened his garden window.

CHRISTOPHER HASSALL *Rupert Brooke*

[B]★

Finally, it is the hope of every modern architect to be instrumental in providing for contemporary society an environment in which the highest aims in commercial, professional, recreational and domestic living can be obtained. Superimposed on these categories is the degree of sophistication implied, the sophistication of multiple functions, varying from the simplest to the most complex, depending on the building's site, be it homestead, village, town, or city. For the architect every design problem is unique and he operates on two levels: utilitarian and aesthetic. Does this mean the scrap-heap for existing buildings expressive of bygone social mores? Not at all. Unless, of course, a building has outgrown its usefulness and has no other merit to command its continued existence. The modern architect has no wish to break continuity with the past, but if he *is* modern nostalgic yearning for, or imitation of, the creative efforts of his predecessors must be ruthlessly forsworn.

JOHN KILLICK *Creed of an Architect*

[C]★

The best confidence builder I know is the really long run, the marathon. If I were not a miler I should like to be a marathon runner, and from time to time have run marathon distances. This introduces you more obviously to what my coach, Percy Cerutty, calls the 'pain reservoir'. In the mile race I have found this comes in about the last two minutes, when pain floods through the body and the only thing you want to do is stop. This is a mental battle as much as a physical one, and it is the runners who can keep going despite this pain who win. During the marathon I find one reaches this pain threshold at about the fifteenth mile, and from then on a voice inside urges one to give up. Cerutty believes that this 'pain reservoir' can be filled only whilst training in pain and be tapped only whilst racing in pain.

Therefore, the more one trains while feeling very tired, the more this reservoir is filled, and, equally important, the more confidence one has in the driving force. I can honestly say that I would never have won a major race without this reservoir. There is a certain animalism in athletics which comes from the efficiency of a well-trained body. But the ability to draw from the pain reservoir is a spiritual quality that comes from all-round training. It is an attitude of mind.

I believe that this is self-discipline, and that it is more valuable than the most carefully-contrived training schedules. I believe further that it carries through to the whole of life, and does not merely apply to athletics. We have to become confident if we are to be any use as men, and nothing builds this confidence better than overcoming the weaknesses to which we are prone.

HERB ELLIOTT *Thoughts on Running*

[D]

Richard turned his reddened eyes towards him. Then he lowered his head. 'You know yourself that the material you sent was full of nonense,' he said in a flat voice. He had suddenly stopped stammering.

'Of that I know nothing,' said Rubashov drily.

'You wrote as if nothing had happened,' said Richard in the same tired voice. 'They beat the Party to shambles, and you just wrote phrases about our unbroken will to victory – the same kind of lies as the communiqués in the Great War. Whoever we showed it to would just spit. You must know all that yourself.'

Rubashov looked at the boy, who now sat leaning forward, elbows on his knees, his chin on his red fists. He answered drily:

'For the second time you ascribe to me an opinion which I do not hold. I must ask you to stop doing so.'

Richard looked at him unbelievingly out of his inflamed eyes. Rubashov went on.

'The Party is going through a severe trial. Other revolutionary parties have been through even more difficult ones. The decisive factor is our unbroken will. Whoever now goes soft and weak does not belong in our ranks. Whoever spreads an atmosphere of panic plays into our enemy's hands. What his motives are in doing so does not make any difference. By his attitude he becomes an enemy to our movement, and will be treated accordingly.'

Richard still sat with his chin in his hands, his face turned to Rubashov.

'So I am a danger to the movement,' he said. 'I play into the enemy's hands. Probably I am paid for doing so. And Anny, too . . .'

'In your pamphlets,' continued Rubashov in the same dry tone of voice, 'of which you admit to be the author, there frequently appear phrases such as this: That we have suffered a defeat, that a catastrophe has befallen the Party, and that we must start afresh and change our policy fundamentally. That is defeatism. It is demoralizing and it lames the Party's fighting spirit.'

'I only know,' said Richard, 'that one must tell people the truth, as they know it already, in any case. It is ridiculous to pretend to them.'

ARTHUR KOESTLER *Darkness at Noon*

[E]

But I do remember one night. A few days before one of my departures by ship from New York. I was with two almost dear friends early on this cold crisp December afternoon. There was a pantry full of Irish whisky. And the air was brimming with Christmas and bright wrappings of presents. One nearly dear friend was a man, the other a woman. Alas,

23

all three of us had escaped from Europe to the new world. We had gone back to our bubbling long cars. Smooth New York State wines. Nights that were all night. And the cultivated utter richness that is New York. I walked tweedily into the pantry. The man friend was talking to the woman friend. They were saying over the tall icy glasses, my God, let's both find a port in this storm. Cuba. Or the Bahamas.

My man friend was wearing sandals and white socks, having broken his shoes kicking some door down in a rage. I had a bandaged arm, torn open having plunged my fist through a window. And this pretty woman looked a thin picture of death. Between the white cupboards of the pantry we stood smiling at each other. They looked at me and said at least you're saved in a few days by the good ship *Franconia*. I said it was true. On that good ship I was going down the North River and out on the cool waters. Next stop Ireland. There was a great friendly clutching of arms and bodies. We were all nearly wailing. She screamed let's find a port quick. And my man friend of course, was taking on fuel. Called Power's Gold Label. In the long drawing-room a madrigal played. Suddenly they were on the telephone, long messages, obscure, confused, to friends back in Europe. And less confused messages to the steamship lines. They were going to escape. We went back into the long room with some sun through the window and lay back on the soft couches.

J. P. DONLEAVY *Whither wigwams*
[from *Meet My Maker the Mad Molecule*]

6
Diction (choice of words)

On completing the critical stages so far described, the critic is ready to begin a close examination of the style, under the headings: diction, imagery, rhythm. In adopting that order, it is not intended to suggest that it is the 'right' or the only order. The individual critic may well choose a different sequence; or at times may vary the order of his own procedures, dealing first with whatever aspect of style makes the sharpest impression at first reading. But, whatever sequence is followed, a passage must be considered under those three headings before a final judgment can be attempted.

In discussing diction, certain basic facts about words and their 'meaning'* must be recalled:

I WORDS ARE NOT THINGS: THEY REFER TO THINGS
When spoken, words are sound waves produced by the speaker's speech organs. When written, they are marks made on paper or other writing material by a pen, pencil, typewriter, printing machine, etc. In either case, words are *symbols* of things, not things themselves. We can usefully distinguish three components of meaning: (i) the symbol or word; (ii) the reference or associations; (iii) the referent or the thing itself, whether concrete or an abstract concept. The word 'means' the thing only because it is associated with it in the mind of the user of the word: a point developed in the following paragraphs.

*The word is quoted to draw attention to the fact that the 'meaning' of the word *meaning* is complex: so complex that some have argued that it should not be used in the discussion of language. Remembering that 'meaning' is *how* something is written as well as *what* is written, we may continue to use the word – cautiously.

II WORDS HAVE MEANING BY ASSOCIATION

Or, put it this way, and as simply as possible: words mean something to us because they are associated with ideas that already exist in our minds. When we use words we do not transmit thoughts directly; we transmit symbols which, we hope, will have for our hearers or readers associations closely corresponding to the associations that the words have for us.

An example will help. If, either in speech or writing, we transmit the symbol *rope* it has 'meaning' for the hearer or reader only in so far as he already has *rope associations* in his mind. Rearrange the letters, and thus alter the symbol, and we transmit the word *pore*. Again, it will have 'meaning' only in so far as the hearer or reader has *pore associations*. Rearrange the letters again, and we transmit the 'meaningless' symbol *roep*. This is intrinsically no more and no less nonsensical than either *rope* or *pore*; but it is, as we say, 'meaningless'–and this because the hearer or reader is extremely unlikely to have *roep associations*.

This principle of meaning through association applies to all the words in our vocabulary and explains how they got there.

III A WORD DOES NOT HAVE ONE, CLEAR, FIXED MEANING

The associations which, for the speaker or writer, are clustered round the symbol that he transmits will hardly ever be identical with the associations that the received symbol arouses in the mind of the hearer or reader. Use of language will, therefore, always vary in efficiency between the two extremes of no communication and almost perfect communication.

In practice, of course, communication is not quite the hit-or-miss business that the preceding paragraph may have appeared to suggest. Most human beings, speaking the same language, have sufficiently similar experiential backgrounds to ensure that–for much of the time at any rate–the word symbols that they employ have common associations. But we do need to remember that words are symbols *not* things, and that identity of meaning through association cannot be assumed. It is notorious, for example, that abstract words such as 'freedom', 'democracy' or 'justice' may mean very different things to different people.

IV WORDS CHANGE THEIR MEANING AS THEIR CONTEXTS CHANGE

A simple example is drawn from headlines: *Red For Danger/ A Dangerous Red*; and it can be argued that in the following sentences the word *tomatoes* has different 'meanings':

Heavy cropping brought down the price of tomatoes in August.
The candidate faced a hostile crowd and was bombarded with tomatoes.

The examples recall R. A. Hall's statement (in *Linguistics and Your Language*): ' . . . the meaning of any linguistic symbol is the situations in which we use it.' Hence the importance of analysing the sense, tone, intention, and the kind of writing before attempting to assess the effectiveness of the diction.

V THE ASSOCIATIONS THAT GIVE A WORD ITS MEANING ARE OF DIFFERENT KINDS

These associations may be described as: (a) sense impressions or 'images'; (b) thoughts or ideas; (c) feelings or emotions. The images and ideas that are associated with a word are called its *reference*. The feelings that are associated with a word are called its *emotive meaning*.

Whether *some* words have purely reference and others purely emotive meaning is a discussion best left to semantics; but even the briefest consideration will show that words can have both kinds of meaning and can be used in such a way as to emphasise either one or the other. *Fascist, capitalism, cricket, hunting, authority, pop music*–these, selected with little effort, illustrate the point; and it would be easy to add to the list. Any one of those words can be used with high or low degree of reference or with high or low degree of emotive meaning. But the examples are offered merely to carry the exposition a stage further, for little is gained by discussing single words in isolation from a meaningful context.

Two people who have watched the same television programme comment quite differently. One says, 'It was a documentary.' The other says, 'It was superb.' The former uses language referentially, and the latter emotively: one provides factual information about the programme, while the other reveals little about the programme but tells us his feelings about the programme.

27

The writer whose concern is primarily with facts uses language referentially; the writer whose concern is primarily with feelings uses language emotively. No absolute distinction is possible between the referential and the emotive (often called the *affective)* use of language. The two blend, and it would be hard to find examples of sustained writing in which the use of words is wholly referential or wholly emotive. A scientist will tend to use language referentially: an orator emotively. Yet the scientist may use words to appeal to the emotions and an orator may use words to convey factual information.

Still, the distinction is of importance to the critic, who should be particularly vigilant in detecting that common abuse of language which occurs, deliberately or accidentally, when emotive meaning is disguised as, or mistaken for, reference. To this topic examples provided later in this section draw particular attention.

Nor should we think of one use of language as being 'better' than the other. Language is used for many purposes. Diction that avoids affective associations is not necessarily superior to language that exploits them. Everything depends upon the writer's aims and upon his skill in adjusting to the particular linguistic situation that his aims create.

VI WORDS CHANGE THEIR MEANING WITH THE PASSAGE OF TIME

This is a fact to bear in mind when criticising the prose of earlier periods. The shift in meaning of the word *nice* between Shakespeare's day and our own is a well-known illustration. Similarly, *wit, science, conceit, atom,* to give only a few further examples, do not now mean what they once did. The critic must try to understand words in the sense intended by the writer, remembering how different may be the associations of a word as used only a century ago from the associations of the 'same' word as used now. The word does not change: its reference may.

In 'creative' works the writer frequently aims to embody keen and accurate observation of people, places, or things in language characterised by precise reference and *at the same time* to employ emotive meaning to communicate his feelings to the reader. Accuracy and clarity of reference together with the emotional appropriateness of the affective language are the marks of successful writing of this kind.

The critic should be sensitive to 'pseudo-emotive' diction: that is, language used emotively but so lacking in precise reference that the reader is being asked to feel strong emotion about nothing in particular. In *East Coker*, T. S. Eliot described such an effect as:

> . . . the general mess of imprecision of feeling,
> Undisciplined squads of emotion.

In such instances the writer is duping the reader into responding emotively to a vague and 'unrealised' object, situation or concept. He is stirring up a vague fog of feeling. In genuine emotive writing the choice of words accurately reflects sharp observation, and the communicated emotion is felt to be inseparable from the *truthful* representation of what is described.

FOR PRACTICE

Note. The critic cannot separate diction from the writer's other stylistic means: imagery and rhythm. Since, however, later sections give detailed consideration to imagery and rhythm, the practical work of this section concentrates on diction. The reader should not on that account feel himself debarred from commenting on striking rhythmic effects or uses of imagery.

1

Read each of the following passages carefully and establish in each case the writer's intentions and the kind of writing. Make comparisons between the passages wherever these are critically helpful–i.e. wherever you are sure that you are comparing passages of a similar kind. (Pay particular attention to tone when deciding to make comparisons.)

2

Comment on the referential or the emotive use of language in the light of each writer's aims.

3

Briefly summarise the argument of each passage.

[A]

I confess that I do not see why the very existence of an in-

invisible world may not in part depend on the personal response which any one of us may make to the religious appeal. God himself, in short, may draw vital strength and increase of very being from our fidelity. For my own part, I do not know what the sweat and blood and tragedy of this life mean, if they mean anything short of this. If this life be not a real fight, in which something is eternally gained for the universe by success, it is no better than a game at private theatricals from which one may withdraw at will. But it *feels* like a real fight, – as if there were something really wild in the universe which we, with all our idealities and faithfulnesses, are needed to redeem; and first of all to redeem our own hearts from atheisms and fears. For such a half-wild, half-saved universe our nature is adapted. The deepest thing in our nature is this dumb region of the heart in which we dwell alone with our willingnesses and unwillingnesses, our faiths and fears. As through the cracks and crannies of caverns those waters exude from the earth's bosom which then form the fountain-heads of springs, so in these crepuscular depths of personality the sources of all our outer deeds and decisions take their rise. Here is our deepest organ of communication with the nature of things; and compared with these concrete movements of our soul all abstract statements and scientific arguments – the veto, for example, which the strict positivist pronounces upon our faith – sound to us like mere chatterings of the teeth.

WILLIAM JAMES *The Will to Believe*

[B]

Only, whereas the passion for doing good is apt to be overhasty in determining what reason and the will of God say, because its turn is for acting rather than thinking, and it wants to be beginning to act; and whereas it is apt to take its own conceptions, which proceed from its own state of development and share in all the imperfections and immaturities of this, for a basis of action; what distinguishes culture is, that is is possessed by the scientific passion as well as by the passion of doing good; that it demands worthy notions and the will of God, and does not readily suffer its own crude conceptions to substitute themselves for them. And knowing that no action or institution can be salutary and stable which is not based on reason and the will of God, it is not so bent on acting and instituting, even with the great aim of diminishing human error and misery ever before its thoughts, but that it can remember that acting and instituting are of little use, unless we know how and what we ought to act and to institute.

MATTHEW ARNOLD *Culture and Anarchy*

[C]

Are we to say then that morality is religion? Most certainly not. In morality the ideal is not: it for ever remains a 'to be'. The reality in us or in the world is partial and inadequate; and no one could say that it answers to the ideal, that, morally considered, both we and the world are all we ought to be, and ought to be just what we are. We have at furthest the belief in an ideal which in its pure completeness is never real; which, as an ideal, is a mere 'should be'. And the question is, Will that do for religion? No knower of religion, who was not led away by a theory, would answer Yes. Nor does it help us to say that religion is 'morality touched by emotion'; for loose phrases of this sort may suggest to the reader what he knows already without their help, but, properly speaking, they *say* nothing. *All* morality is, in one sense or another, 'touched by emotion'. Most emotions, high or low, can go with and 'touch' morality; and the moment we leave our phrase-making, and begin to reflect, we see all that is meant is that morality 'touched' by *religious* emotion is religious; and so, as answer to the question What is religion? all that we have said is, 'It is religion when with morality you have–religion.' I do not think we learn a very great deal from this.

F. H. BRADLEY *Ethical Studies*

[D]

Man may be excused for feeling some pride at having risen, though not through his own exertions, to the very summit of the organic scale; and the fact of his having thus risen, instead of having been aboriginally placed there, may give him hopes for a still higher destiny in the distant future. But we are not here concerned with hopes or fears, only with the truth as far as our reason allows us to discover it. I have given the evidence to the best of my ability; and we must acknowledge, as it seems to me, that man with all his noble qualities, with sympathy which feels for the most debased, with benevolence which extends not only to other men but to the humblest living creature, with his god-like intellect which has penetrated into the movements and constitution of the solar system – with all these exalted powers – Man still bears in his bodily frame the indelible stamp of his lowly origin.

CHARLES DARWIN *The Descent of Man*

[E]

I am a zoologist and the naked ape is an animal. He is therefore fair game for my pen and I refuse to avoid him simply because some of his behaviour patterns are rather complex and impressive. My excuse is that, in becoming so erudite, *Homo sapiens* has remained a naked ape nevertheless; in acquiring lofty new motives, he has lost none of the earthy old ones. This is frequently a cause of some embarrassment to him, but his old impulses have been with him for millions of years, his new ones only a few thousand at the most – and there is no hope of quickly shrugging off the accumulated genetic legacy of his whole evolutionary past. He would be a far less worried and more fulfilled animal if only he would face up to this fact. Perhaps this is where the zoologist can help.

DESMOND MORRIS *The Naked Ape*

4

Establish the common and contrasting features of the following passages, paying particular attention to tone and intention. Describe the kind of writing in each case.

5

Bearing in mind the critical guidelines established in answering question 4, discuss each writer's use of referential and emotive diction, paying particular attention to clarity of reference and the emotional appropriateness of the affective language. Support your comments with brief quotations.

6

Which of these writers is least successful in achieving his aims, and why?

[A]

Mary had turned into a full-grown damsel, comely, sweet, and graceful. She was tall enough never to look short, and short enough never to seem too tall, even when her best feelings were outraged; and nobody, looking at her face, could wish to do anything but please her; so kind was the gaze of her deep blue eyes, so pleasant the frankness of her gentle forehead, so playful the readiness of rosy lips for a pretty answer or a lovely smile. But if any could be found so callous and morose as not to be charmed or nicely cheered by this, let him only take a longer look, not rudely, but simply in a spirit of polite inquiry; and then would he see, on the delicate rounding of each soft and dimpled cheek, a carmine hard to match on pallet, morning sky, or flower-bed. . . .

The buoyant power and brilliance of the morning are upon her, and the air of the bright sea lifts and spreads her, like a pillowy skate's egg. The polish of the wet sand flickers, like veneer of maple-wood, at every quick touch of her dancing feet. Her dancing feet are as light as nature and high spirits made them, not even quit of spindle heels but even free from shoes and socks left high and dry on the shingle. And lighter even than the dancing feet the merry heart is dancing, laughing at the shadows of its own delight; while the radiance of blue eyes springs, like a fount of brighter heaven; and the sunny hair falls, flows, or floats, to provoke the wind for playmate.

Such a pretty sight was good to see for innocence and large-ness. So the buoyancy of nature springs anew in those who have been weary, when they see her brisk power inspiring the young, who never stand still to think of her, but are up and away with her, where she will, at the breath of her subtle encouragement.

R. D. BLACKMORE *Mary Anerley*

[B]

Above green-flashing plunges of a weir, and shaken by the thunder below, lilies, golden and white, were swaying at anchor among the reeds. Meadow-sweet hung from the banks thick with weed and trailing bramble, and there also hung a daughter of earth. Her face was shaded by a broad straw hat with a flexible brim that left her lips and chin in the sun, and, sometimes nodding, sent forth a light of promising eyes. Across her shoulders, and behind, flowed large loose curls, brown in shadow, almost golden where the ray touched them. . . . The little skylark went up above her, all song, to the smooth southern cloud lying along the blue: from a dewy copse dark over her nodding hat the blackbird fluted, calling to her with thrice mellow note: the kingfisher flashed emerald out of green osiers; a bow-winged heron travelled aloft, seeking solitude: a boat slipped towards her, containing a dreamy youth; and still she plucked her fruit and ate, and mused, as if no fairy prince were invading her territories, and as if she wished not for one, or knew not her wishes. Sur-rounded by the green shaven meadows, the pastoral summer buzz, the weirfall's thundering white, amid the breath and beauty of wild flowers, she was a bit of lovely human life in a setting: a terrible attraction.

GEORGE MEREDITH *The Ordeal of Richard Feverel*

[C]

In the evening, when the milking was finished, and all the things fed, then we went out to look at the snares. We wandered on across the stream and up the wild hill-side. Our feet rattled through black patches of devil's-bit scabious; we skirted a swim of thistle-down, which glistened when the moon touched it. We stumbled on through wet, coarse grass, over soft molehills and black rabbit-holes. The hills and woods cast shadows; the pools of mist in the valleys gathered the moonbeams in cold, shivery light.

We came to an old farm that stood on the level brow of the hill. The woods swept away from it, leaving a great clearing of what was once cultivated land. The handsome chimneys of the house, silhouetted against a light sky, drew my admiration. I noticed that there was no light or glow from any window, though the house had only the width of one room, and though the night was only at eight o'clock. We looked at the long, impressive front. Several of the windows had been bricked in, giving a pitiful impression of blindness; the places where the plaster had fallen off the walls showed blacker in the shadow. We pushed open the gate, and as we walked down the path, weeds and dead plants brushed our ankles. We looked in at a window. The room was lighted also by a window from the other side, through which the moonlight streamed on to the flagged floor, dirty, littered with paper and wisps of straw. The hearth lay in the light, with all its distress of grey ashes, and piled cinders of burnt paper, and a child's headless doll, charred and pitiful. On the border-line of shadow lay a round fur cap – a gamekeeper's cap. I blamed the moonlight for entering the desolate room; the darkness alone was decent and reticent. I hated the little roses on the illuminated piece of wall-paper, I hated that fireside.

With farmer's instinct George turned to the outhouse. The cow-yard startled me. It was a forest of the tallest nettles I had ever seen – nettles far taller than my six feet. The air was soddened with the dank scent of nettles. As I followed George along the obscure brick path, I felt my flesh creep. But the buildings, when we entered them, were in splendid condition; they had been restored within a small number of years; they were well-timbered, neat, and cosy. Here and there we saw feathers, bits of animal wreckage, even the remnants of a cat, which we hastily examined by the light of a match. As we entered the stable there was an ugly noise, and three great rats half rushed at us and threatened us with their vicious teeth. I shuddered, and hurried back, stumbling over a bucket, rotten with rust, and so filled with weeds that I thought it part of the jungle. There was a silence made horrible by the faint noises that rats and flying bats give out. The place was bare of any vestige of corn or straw or hay, only choked with a growth of abnormal weeds. When I found myself free in the orchard I could not stop shivering. There were no apples to be seen overhead between us and the clear sky. Either the birds had caused them to fall, when the rabbits had devoured them, or someone had gathered the crop.

'This,' said George bitterly, 'is what the Mill will come to.'

D. H. LAWRENCE *The White Peacock*

7

The writer of one of the following passages had very different aims from the other two. What features of the diction enable you to prove this? Support your answer with examples.

8

If you think that you detect pseudo-emotive writing in any of these passages pick out and analyse some examples.

9

Judge the effectiveness of each passage in relation to the writer's aims.

[A]

By daylight, the bower of Oak's new-found mistress, Bathsheba Everdene, presented itself as a hoary building, of the early stage of Classic Renaissance as regards its architecture, and of a proportion which told at a glance that, as is so frequently the case, it had once been the manorial hall upon a small estate around it, now altogether effaced as a distinct property, and merged in the vast tract of a non-resident landlord, which comprised several such modest demesnes.

Fluted pilasters, worked from the solid stone, decorated its front, and above the roof the chimneys were panelled or columnar, some coped gables with finials and like features still retaining traces of their Gothic extraction. Soft brown mosses, like faded velveteen, formed cushions upon the stone tiling, and tufts of the houseleek or sengreen sprouted from the eaves of the low surrounding buildings. A gravel walk leading from the door to the road in front was encrusted at the sides with more moss—here it was a silver-green variety, the nut-brown of the gravel being visible to the width of only a foot or two in the centre. This circumstance, and the generally sleepy air of the whole prospect here, together with the animated and contrasting state of the reverse facade, suggested to the imagination that on the adaptation of the building for farming purposes the vital principle of the house had turned round inside its body to face the other way. Reversals of this kind, strange deformities, tremendous paralyses, are often seen to be inflicted by trade upon edifices— either individual or in the aggregate as streets and towns— which were once planned for pleasure alone.

Lively voices were heard this morning in the upper rooms, the main staircase to which was of hard oak, the balusters, heavy as bed-posts, being turned and moulded in the quaint fashion of their century, the handrail as stout as a parapet-top, and the stairs themselves continually twisting round like a person trying to look over his shoulder. Going up, the floors above were found to have a very irregular surface, rising to ridges, sinking into valleys; and being just then uncarpeted, the face of the boards was seen to be eaten into innumerable vermiculations. Every window replied by a clang to the opening and shutting of every door, a tremble followed every bustling movement, and a creak accompanied a walker about the house, like a spirit, wherever he went.

In the room from which the conversation proceeded, Bathsheba and her servant-companion, Liddy Smallbury, were to be discovered sitting upon the floor, and sorting a complication of papers, books, bottles, and rubbish spread out thereon–remnants from the household stores of the late occupier. Liddy, the maltster's great-granddaughter, was about Bathsheba's equal in age, and her face was a prominent advertisement of the light-hearted English country girl. The beauty her features might have lacked in form was amply made up for by perfection of hue, which at this winter-time was the softened ruddiness on a surface of high rotundity that we meet with in a Terburg or a Gerard Douw; and, like the presentations of those great colourists, it was a face which kept well back from the boundary between comeliness and the ideal. Though elastic in nature she was less daring than Bathsheba, and occasionally showed some earnestness, which consisted half of genuine feeling, and half of mannerliness superadded by way of duty.

THOMAS HARDY *Far From The Madding Crowd*

[B]

Now they had left the high-road and were making south-east through the winding lanes. Their shoulders were turned to the sea, though in that lost world of the mist only the native could tell where the bay was supposed to lie. It was one of those dead hours, too, when even the salt goes out of the marsh-air, and no pulse in it warns you subconsciously of the miracle coming. Between the high-mounted hedges it was still and close, and beyond them the land rose until its dark green surface stood soft against the sky. All the way Simon looked at the land with a critical eye, the eye of a lover which loves and asks at the same time. He looked at the ploughland and knew the rotation through which it had run and would have to run again; at the rich grass-land which seemed never to have known the steel, and fields which, at rest for a hundred years, still spoke to some long-rusted share. He loved it, but he thought of it first and foremost as good material for the good workman engaged on the only job in the world. It was always the land that he coveted when he came to Blindbeck, never the house. Eliza had made of the house a temple to the god of blessed self-satisfaction, but even Eliza could not spoil the honest, workable land.

The farm kept showing itself to them as they drove, a quadrangle of long, well-kept buildings backed by trees. When the sun shone, the white faces of house and shippon looked silver through the peeping-holes of the hedge, but to-day they were wan and ghostly in the deadening mist. The turned beeches and chestnuts were merely rusty, instead of glowing, and seemed to droop as if with the weight of moisture on their boughs. The Scotch firs on a mound alone, stark, straight, aloof, had more than ever that air of wild freedom which they carry into the tamest country; and the pearly shadow misting their green alike in wet weather or in dry, was today the real mist, of which they always wear the other in remembrance.

The farm had its back well into the grassy hill, and the blind river which gave it its name wound its way down to it in a hidden channel and went away from it in a hidden dip in a field below. There was water laid on at Blindbeck, as Sarah knew, with a copper cylinder in a special linen-room, and a hot towel-rail and a porcelain bath. Simon's particular envy was the electric light, that marvel of marvels on a northern farm. He never got over the wonder of putting his hand to the switch, and seeing the light flash out on the second to his call. Once he had sneaked out of the house on a winter's night, and in the great shippon had turned the lights on full. Eliza, of course, had been nasty about it when she had heard, but Will had understood him and had only laughed. Later, swinging a lantern in his own dark shippon, Simon had thought of those switches with envious longing. He did not know that they had taken the warm glamour out of the place, and slain at a blow the long tradition of its beauty. The lantern went with him like a descended star as he moved about, and out of the cattle's breath wove for itself gold-dusted haloes. There had been something precious about it all before, some sense of mystery and long-garnered peace, but to-night he could only remember Blindbeck and its modern toy. For the time being he ceased to feel the pull of the sweetest chain in the world, which runs straight back through all the ages to the Child in the Bethlehem Stall. . . .

CONSTANCE HOLME *The Splendid Fairing*

[C]

Dawn crept over the Downs like a sinister white animal, followed by the snarling cries of a wind eating its way between the black boughs of the thorns. The wind was the furious voice of this sluggish animal light that was baring the dormers and mullions and scullions of Cold Comfort Farm.

The farm was crouched on a bleak hill-side, whence its fields, fanged with flints, dropped steeply to the village of Howling a mile away. Its stables and out-houses were built in the shape of a rough octangle surrounding the farmhouse itself, which was built in the shape of a rough triangle. The left point of the triangle abutted on the farthest point of the octangle, which was formed by the cowsheds, which lay parallel with the big barn. The out-houses were built of rough-cast stone, with thatched roofs, while the farm itself was partly built of local flint, set in cement, and partly of some stone brought at great trouble and enormous expense from Perthshire.

The farmhouse was a long, low building, two-storied in parts. Other parts of it were three-storied. Edward the Sixth had originally owned it in the form of a shed in which he housed his swineherds, but he had grown tired of it, and had rebuilt it, in Sussex clay. Then he pulled it down. Elizabeth had rebuilt it, with a good many chimneys in one way and another. The Charleses had let it alone; but William and Mary had pulled it down again, and George the First had rebuilt it.

George the Second, however, burned it down. George the Third added another wing. George the Fourth pulled it down again.

By the time England began to develop that magnificent blossoming of trade and imperial expansion which fell to her lot under Victoria, there was not much of the original building left, save the tradition that it had always been there. It crouched, like a beast about to spring, under the bulk of Mock-uncle Hill. Like ghosts embedded in brick and stone, the architectural variations of each period through which it had passed were mute history. It was known locally as 'The King's Whim'.

The front door of the farm faced a perfectly inaccessible ploughed field at the back of the house; it had been the whim of Red Raleigh Starkadder, in 1835, to have it so; and so the family always used to come in by the back door, which abutted on the general yard facing the cowsheds. A long corridor ran half-way through the house on the second story and then stopped. One could not get into the attics at all. It was all very awkward.

Growing with the viscous light that was invading the sky, there came the solemn, tortured-snake voice of the sea, two miles away, falling in sharp folds upon the mirror-expanses of the beach.

Under the ominous bowl of the sky a man was ploughing the sloping field immediately below the farm, where the flints shone bone-sharp and white in the growing light. The ice-cascade of the wind leaped over him, as he guided the plough over the flinty runnels. Now and again he called roughly to his team:

'Upidee, Travail! Ho, there, Arsenic! Jug-jug!' But for the most part he worked in silence, and silent were his team. The light showed no more of his face than a grey expanse of flesh, expressionless as the land he ploughed, from which looked out two sluggish eyes.

Every now and again, when he came to the corner of the

field and was forced to tilt the scranlet of his plough almost on to its axle to make the turn, he glanced up at the farm where it squatted on the gaunt shoulder of the hill, and something like a possessive gleam shone in his dull eyes. But he only turned his team again, watching the crooked passage of the scranlet through the yeasty earth, and muttered: 'Hola, Arsenic! Belay there, Travail!' while the bitter light waned into full day.

STELLA GIBBONS *Cold Comfort Farm*

7
Imagery

Basically, imagery is a verbal appeal to the reader's sense perceptions. Whenever a writer uses words that awaken in the reader's memory or imagination a concept of the senses of touch, taste, smell, sight, hearing, or movement, he is using an image. We can, therefore, classify images according to the sense perception to which they appeal: sight (visual images of colour or shape); hearing (audile images); taste (gustatory images); smell (olfactory images); touch (thermal or tactile images); movement (kinaesthetic images).*

I DESCRIPTIVE IMAGERY
The function of an image may be mainly descriptive; and this function will be unaffected by the simplicity or elaboration of the image. At its most rudimentary, the descriptive image may be 'vestigial'. Descriptive words such as colour adjectives or concrete nouns, for example, contain a 'built-in' or 'fossilised' sense perception (red, blue, apple, house, horse) but are not usually thought of as images or treated as such in criticism. Attempt FOR PRACTICE 1 on page 55.

II SYMBOLIC IMAGERY
The sense perceptions stirred to life in the reader's memory or imagination by the writer's image may themselves symbolise emotions and/or ideas. If this happens, then the function of the image is *symbolic*.†

*There is no need to use the formal terms, but it is useful to know them.
†The diagram oversimplifies a complex process, but helps to clarify thinking about an important critical point.

43

It is impossible to draw an absolute distinction between the descriptive and the symbolic use of imagery, for descriptive images always carry with them associated – if vestigial – feelings and ideas, and symbolic images cannot exist without a descriptive element. Yet a distinction can be made between the mainly symbolic and the mainly descriptive. For many writers imagery is a major means of arousing emotions and ideas appropriate to their subject matter and reinforceful of their purposes. They seek to fuse with the sense perception element of their images an emotional and intellectual complex harmonious with their overall aim and apt to their immediate purpose.

To oversimplify again, we may say that where the image is mainly descriptive its effectiveness is limited to its sensuous element. Where the image is mainly symbolic its power resides in the emotional and intellectual complex that it transmits via its sensuous element.

Discussing symbolic imagery, Coleridge wrote in *Biographia Literaria*: 'the balance or reconcilement . . . of . . . the idea with the image' is one of the surest marks of 'that power to which I would exclusively appropriate the name Imagination'.

An understanding of the working of symbolic imagery is especially important when the critic is confronted with 'modern' prose – roughly post-1900.

EXAMPLE WITH COMMENTARY

The following passage from Virginia Woolf's *To the Lighthouse* makes explicit the way in which symbolic imagery does its work. Two of the characters, Lily Briscoe and William Bankes, are walking together and discussing a third character, Mr Ramsay:

'Oh but,' said Lily, 'think of his work!'

Whenever she 'thought of his work' she always saw clearly before her a large kitchen table. It was Andrew's doing. She asked him what his father's books were about. 'Subject and object and the nature of reality,' Andrew had said. And when she said Heavens, she had no notion what that meant. 'Think of a kitchen table then,' he told her, 'when you're not there.'

So she always saw, when she thought of Mr Ramsay's work, a scrubbed kitchen table. It lodged now in the fork of a pear tree, for they had reached the orchard. And with a painful effort of concentration, she focused her mind, not upon the silver-bossed bark of the tree, or upon its fish-shaped leaves, but upon a phantom kitchen table, one of those scrubbed board tables, grained and knotted, whose virtue seems to have been laid bare by years of muscular integrity, which stuck there, its four legs in air. Naturally, if one's days were passed in this seeing of angular essences, this reducing of lovely evenings, with all their flamingo clouds and blue and silver to a white deal four-legged table (and it was a mark of the finest minds so to do), naturally one could not be judged like an ordinary person.

1 The passage traces the origin and the development of the symbolic image – 'the large kitchen table' – which, in Lily Briscoe's mind, 'stands for' (or symbolises) Mr Ramsay's work. His son Andrew, asked to explain the nature of his father's books, had given Lily a 'concept definition' ('subject and object and the nature of reality') which she did not understand. He then tried to illustrate his father's speculations about the nature of reality by inviting her to 'think of a kitchen table when you're not there' (his way of making concrete the philosophical speculation about whether an object exists independently of an observer); but he could, just as appropriately to his purposes, have instanced a rosebush, or a house, or a tree, or any other concrete object. For Lily, however, the object he chose as his illustration triggered off an explosion of associations: *scrubbed– scrubbed board – grained and knotted – virtue . . . laid bare by years of muscular integrity*. (Trace through the rest of the passage the further development of the symbolism.) It is plain that the image is intended to communicate to the reader not so much Lily Briscoe's rather vague ideas about the nature of Mr Ramsay's work as her strong feelings and ideas about Mr Ramsay himself. Note how Mr Ramsay – identified with the clearly realised and objectively described table – intrudes upon and 'reduces' the beauty of the scene, thus conveying a great deal both about Lily Briscoe and about him, as he affects her.

2 The difference between mainly symbolic imagery and mainly

descriptive imagery is illustrated in the passage. Compare the function of the kitchen table image with that of the 'silver-bossed bark' and the 'fish-shaped leaves'.

3 In Section 6 it was stressed that successful emotive writing is based on precision of reference. Find and discuss examples in this passage.

4 The 'theme image' in this passage illustrates the fusion of the idea with the image, to recall Coleridge's point, already quoted. An image has three elements:

(*a*) the thing talked about, or the *tenor*;

(*b*) the thing to which it is compared, or the *vehicle*;

(*c*) the features common to both, or the *ground*.

In the 'kitchen table image' in this passage, the tenor is ostensibly Mr Ramsay's work, but—as we have seen—he himself is really the tenor. The vehicle is the kitchen table. The power and truth of the image can be fully realised only by working out in detail its ground–i.e. by noting the numerous points at which the tenor and the vehicle coincide in common features.

5 Imagery, as has been stated, is a means to an end and is to be judged as such. In this passage the writer's chief purpose is to establish a contrast between Lily Briscoe's 'artistic' impulse and Mr Ramsay's 'rational' approach to life. Note how the images, symbolic and descriptive, are grouped: silver-bossed bark, fish-shaped leaves, flamingo clouds, blue and silver . . . etc; scrubbed board tables, angular essences, white deal four-legged table . . . etc.

Close study of imagery and description as used in the text will show how the context charges both with extra power by the interactions deliberately set up. The 'clustering' of the images into two contrasting groups emphasises the hostility between Mr Ramsay and Lily and between the life values that each represents. Such manipulation of detail within the total context to procure a continuous reaction between contrasting and comparable elements is one of the surest marks of high creative skill.

III DIRECT AND INDIRECT EXPRESSION

As it is important to distinguish between the mainly descriptive and the mainly symbolical use of imagery, so another broad distinction may usefully be made—that between *direct* and *indirect* expression,★ imagery generally having little if any part to play in the former.

The combination of all these causes forms so great a mass of influences hostile to Individuality, that it is not easy to see how it can stand its ground. It will do so with increasing difficulty, unless the intelligent part of the public can be made to feel its value—to see that it is good there should be differences, even though not for the better, even though, as it may appear to them, some should be for the worse. If the claims of Individuality are ever to be asserted, the time is now, while much is wanting to complete the enforced assimilation. It is only in the earlier stages that any stand can be successfully made against the encroachment. The demand that all other people shall resemble ourselves, grows by what it feeds on. If resistance waits till life is reduced *nearly* to one uniform type, all deviations from that type will come to be considered impious, immoral, even monstrous and contrary to nature. Mankind speedily become unable to conceive diversity, when they have been for some time unaccustomed to see it.

JOHN STUART MILL On Liberty

That is an example of extreme directness of expression. There is no doubt that Mill cared deeply about his subject, but in the text quoted his purpose was to make, clearly and persuasively, a direct statement of his ideas.

So, too, a prose writer may be concerned to make a clear, direct statement of facts and/or of his emotions about the facts—without employing imagery.

You know we are speaking always of the real, active, continual, national worship; that by which men act, while they live; not that which they talk of, when they die. Now, we have, indeed, a nominal religion, to which we pay tithes of property and sevenths of time; but we have also a practical

---

★See *Poetry Direct and Oblique* by E. M. W. Tillyard for a stimulating discussion of this distinction as applied to poetry.

and earnest religion, to which we devote nine-tenths of our property, and six-sevenths of our time. And we dispute a great deal about the nominal religion: but we are all unanimous about this practical one; of which I think you will admit that the ruling goddess may be best generally described as the 'Goddess of Getting-on' or 'Britannia of the Market'. The Athenians had an 'Athena Agoraia', or Athena of the Market; but she was a subordinate type of their goddess, while our Britannia Agoraia is the principal type of ours. And all your great architectural works are, of course, built to her. It is long since you built a great cathedral; and how you would laugh at me if I proposed building a cathedral on the top of one of these hills of yours, to make it an Acropolis! But your railroad mounds, vaster than the walls of Babylon; your railroad stations, vaster than the temple of Ephesus, and innumerable; your chimneys, how much more mighty and costly than cathedral spires! your harbour-piers; your warehouses; your exchanges!—all these are built to your great Goddess of 'Getting-on'; and she has formed, and will continue to form, your architecture, as long as you worship her; and it is quite vain to ask me to tell you how to build to *her*; you know far better than I.

JOHN RUSKIN *The Crown of Wild Olive*

It may be argued that there is what might be called 'fossilised imagery' in that text ('. . . the walls of Babylon . . .'; '. . . your harbour-piers . . .'; 'vaster than the temple of Ephesus . . .') but such—to use the more common term—'vestigial images' hardly affect our description of this text as an imageless passage, purposed to present the facts as Ruskin saw them and his emotions about them, with a view to persuading his audience into a new attitude.

Indirect expression, on the other hand, commonly depends much upon imagery, descriptive or symbolic, for its impact. Two main methods may be noted. The writer may employ direct statement of fact, but convey his experience of those facts indirectly and largely through imagery.

My walk home was lengthened by a diversion in the direction of the kirk. When beneath its walls, I perceived decay had made progress, even in seven months—many a window showed black gaps deprived of glass; and slates jutted off, here and there, beyond the right line of the roof, to be gradually worked off in coming autumn storms.

I sought, and soon discovered, the three head-stones on the slope next the moor—the middle one, grey, and half buried in heath—Edgar Linton's only harmonised by the turf, and moss creeping up its foot—Heathcliff's still bare.

I lingered round them, under that benign sky; watched the moths fluttering among the heath, and the hare-bells; listened to the soft wind breathing through the grass; and wondered how any one could ever imagine unquiet slumbers, for the sleepers in that quiet earth.

EMILY BRONTË *Wuthering Heights*

1 That text repays close examination. In the first paragraph facts are directly stated, the description depending little on imagery—such images as there are being vestigial ('. . . black gaps . . .') and mainly descriptive. The effect of the paragraph as a whole, however, is not entirely pictorial, for the storm-battered church stirs a strong emotional response.

2 In the second paragraph, again, direct description and vestigial images go together; but again the description carries strong emotional overtones: the three graves are each merging gradually into the moorland scene and lie near to a church which—as paragraph one described—is itself succumbing to nature.

3 In the last paragraph the full force of the indirectness of the writing is revealed; and the final clause makes explicit what we had earlier suspected—that the real content of the text is not the directly expressed facts, but the narrator's implied emotions about them. (Note, for example, how 'benign sky' and 'the soft wind' anticipate the 'wonderings' of the last clause.)

The analysis just offered is a mere outline. It points the way towards a full critical examination of the interplay of the descriptive elements employed in the text and of the interlocking of the descriptive functions of each of the three paragraphs. And, of course, the text is itself but a fragment of a novel, drawing strength and point from a total context that would be reckoned with in any sustained criticism. Such a critical study might well reveal that these three paragraphs, with their counterpointed tensions, together constitute a symbolic image in which the 'meaning' of the novel is represented.

But we may be content for the moment with observing that, though the immediate impression made by a text may be one of directness of expression, its true purpose may be indirect; and that in attaining such an effect the carefully contrived relationships between descriptive and symbolic elements will be of critical importance.

The second method open to the writer is to use imagery to express indirectly both the facts and his experience of the facts.

In the following passage from James Joyce's *Portrait of the Artist as a Young Man* the imagery used in the third paragraph serves this twofold purpose: the experience itself and Stephen Dedalus's encounter with it are fused. There is no separating the two. In this respect, contrast Joyce's use of imagery in the other paragraphs, where—though descriptive and symbolic elements may both be found—the method is that described earlier: direct expression of the facts and indirect expression of the experience.

There was no human figure near him nor any sound borne to him over the air. But the tide was near the turn and already the day was on the wane. He turned landward and ran towards the shore and, running up the sloping beach, reckless of the sharp shingle, found a sandy nook amid a ring of tufted sandknolls and lay down there that the peace and silence of the evening might still the riot of his blood.

He felt above him the vast indifferent dome and the calm processes of the heavenly bodies; and the earth beneath him, the earth that had borne him, had taken him to her breast.

He closed his eyes in the langour of sleep. His eyelids trembled as if they felt the vast cyclic movement of the earth and her watchers, trembled as if they felt the strange light of some new world. His soul was swooning into some new world, fantastic, dim, uncertain as under sea, traversed by cloudy shapes and beings. A world, a glimmer or a flower? Glimmering and trembling, trembling and unfolding, a breaking light, an opening flower, it spread in endless succession to itself, breaking in full crimson and unfolding and fading to palest rose, leaf by leaf and wave of light by wave of light, flooding all the heavens with its soft flushes, every flush deeper than the other.

Evening had fallen when he woke and the sand and arid grasses of his bed glowed no longer. He rose slowly and, recalling the rapture of his sleep, sighed at its joy.

He climbed to the crest of the sandhill and gazed about him. Evening had fallen. A rim of the young moon cleft the pale waste of skyline, the rim of a silver hoop embedded in grey sand; and the tide was flowing in fast to the land with a low whisper of her waves, islanding a few last figures in distant pools.

Note the changes in method. In paragraph 1 the imagery is strongly sensuous and mainly descriptive. The expression is, therefore, direct; but with emotional overtones. In paragraph 2 the images are vestigial ('dome . . . heavenly bodies . . . earth beneath him . . .'). They contrast strongly with the sensuousness of the first paragraph, and Joyce here makes a plain direct statement of Stephen's experience. In paragraph 3 both the dream-experience and Stephen's experience of it are simultaneously implied through the images. In paragraph 4 direct statement returns as Stephen awakes and recalls the dream rapture. Paragraph 5 resembles the first paragraph in its method, though the mood evoked by the descriptive images is very different: note the starkness of the final image and the evocation of a sense of isolation. Now attempt FOR PRACTICE 2 on page 57.

IV IMAGE CLUSTERS

It was stated earlier that imagery is one of the means whereby the prose writer tries to attain his ends. Like diction and rhythm, it serves his purposes; and there would thus be little point in merely classifying the images in a given text according to the sense perceptions to which they appeal. The critic's task is always to identify and analyse in order to judge the effectiveness of a writer's chosen means in relation to his ends. But the habit of classifying images is useful to the critic in so far as it leads to greater awareness of the writer's purposes. The use of *image clusters*, for example, often signals the presence of emotional and/or intellectual themes that are central to the writer's intentions. Both the passages in FOR PRACTICE 3 may be profitably studied as examples of the cumulative and 'thematic' effect that can be achieved through the sustained use of linked images.

When considering the text from Virginia Woolf (pp. 44–45), attention was directed to the importance of a fusion between *tenor* (the thing talked about) and *vehicle* (the thing to which it is compared). Her 'kitchen table image' was found successful by reason of the numerous points of coincidence between those two elements in the common *ground* in which they were bedded by her imagination.

The point holds good both for the individual image and for the relationship between each individual image and the total context provided by the passage. Consider in the light of this comment, the sustained similes in the passage from *Yeast*, FOR PRACTICE 3.

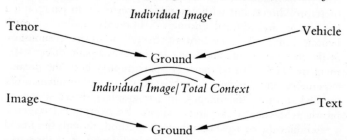

Of course, to achieve a given effect, a writer may *deliberately* use a clashing image; one that juts dramatically out of the text, drawing attention to itself by reason of its unlikeness and singularity. The effect will be particularly striking – for better or worse – in a passage marked by the cumulative force of image clusters.

V THE SOURCES OF IMAGERY

The critic may sometimes gain valuable insights by studying the sources from which a writer draws his images; and such an approach, commonly adopted nowadays in the criticism of drama and poetry, may be fruitful in the criticism of prose, as the examples in FOR PRACTICE 4 show.

VI PUBLIC AND PRIVATE IMAGERY

Further consideration of Virginia Woolf's 'kitchen table image' leads to an important critical distinction: between 'public' and 'private' imagery. In the text quoted from *To The Lighthouse* the writer was careful to show the origin and formation of that particular symbolic image in Lily Briscoe's mind. We were given its source: Andrew Ramsay's suggestion that she should 'think of a kitchen table when you are not there'. We saw, too, how the tenor of the image shifted from being Mr Ramsay's work to being Lily Briscoe's thoughts and feelings about Mr Ramsay himself. Consequently, we had no difficulty in responding to the image: we knew what it 'meant', both intellectually and emotionally.

Writers do not, however, always give us such help. 'Difficult' images may be used with little or no 'explanation', and the critic—especially of modern work–must frequently encounter this problem of obscurity. Typical of the situation would be, but in isolation, the last sentence of the Virginia Woolf text:

Naturally, if one's days were passed in this seeing of angular essences, this reducing of lovely evenings, with all their flamingo clouds and blue and silver to a white deal four-legged table (and it was a mark of the finest minds so to do), naturally one could not be judged like an ordinary person.

To some extent, of course, the problem is inherent in the nature of language. Words, as we have seen, acquire their 'meaning' through association; and images are made of words. No two people have identical word associations. Again, sense perceptions differ from individual to individual; no two people have precisely the same experiential background; nor are their reading, their learning, their intelligence identical. Such, briefly, is the area within which imagery operates, endowed with enormous potential power, but a power accompanied by inherent dangers.

The modern writer, more self-consciously than his predecessors, is concerned with what Virginia Woolf called the 'significant instant'. To communicate both the instant and its significance, he relies very largely upon imagery. He seeks, through imagery, to recreate within his reader's mind his own fleeting visions of truth, perceptions of reality, 'epiphanies' ('manifestations of divinity') – all these, and many more such terms, have been employed to describe such mystical experiences, linking the beholder to the object beheld, and through the consequent awareness of harmony establishing, if only momentarily, a permanence within the flux of experience – a resolution of the tensions imposed by life. It is again from the writing of Virginia Woolf that we can best illustrate the way in which the writer conceives of the operation of imagery to achieve this symbolic communication of what, by its very nature, is barely communicable. She describes the elements of the image as being *brought purposely together to assemble outwardly the scattered parts of the vision within.*

Enough, perhaps, has been said to indicate the delicacy of the critic's task. And in no critical area will that delicacy be more tested than in drawing a just and perceptive distinction between 'public' and 'private' imagery. The terms are used to distinguish between the image that comes home to the general reader and the image that fails to make the desired impact because it lacks universality. It is restricted by origin or in use – and, finally, in significance – to a small circle, an in-group.

The critic, faced with obscurity of imagery (or, of course, of diction) must, before condemning, be sure that the fault does not lie with him. His reception of the text (see Section 5) should have removed some possible causes of difficulty: hasty or unsympathetic reading; prejudice against either content or style. There may well remain difficulties that are the fault of neither the writer nor the reader: for example, images drawn from a markedly different reading background. An extreme instance of this would be the case of a writer versed in the classical literature of Greece or Rome and a reader widely read in the sciences but knowing little of Greek or Latin history, literature, myth or legend. An illustration may be drawn from poetry: many admirers of Yeats's later work find the early poems difficult because of their frequent allusions to Irish legends; yet in a deeper sense the later poems are much more 'difficult', because more profound, than the earlier.

Profundity of subject matter and thought may indeed—and obviously—be a source of image difficulty. As critics, we must allow for this, just as we must expect a creative writer to presume upon his reader's willingness to approach what he has written with an open and unprejudiced mind. He may, too, be allowed to hope that his reader possesses imaginative faculties which, stirred by the creativity of the artist, will quicken and deepen. The writer will often demand that we bring to his work a readiness to experiment; a willingness and a capacity to think and feel quickly and simultaneously; a spontaneity of response which will not insist on the dotting of every *i* and the crossing of every *t*. Intellectual and emotional cross-references; the comparison of things that we have habitually considered unlike; the establishment of new sympathies; the development of our sensibilities and of our sense perceptions—all these will at once be demanded of us and conferred upon us when we encounter that fusion of idea with image which is the distinctive mark of the highest imaginative faculty.

The true critic works in harmony with the writer and responds to the demands that art makes upon him. Yet he must be vigilant to detect and to condemn wilful obscurity, mere cleverness of imagery, vague reference and pseudo-emotive appeal.

FOR PRACTICE

1

Classify the images (including the vestigial images) in this extract.

The traveller, descending from the slopes of Luna, even as he got his first view of the *Port-of-Venus*, would pause by the way, to read the face, as it were, of so beautiful a dwelling-place, lying away from the white road, at the point where it began to decline somewhat steeply to the marsh-land below. The building of pale red and yellow marble, mellowed by age, which he saw beyond the gates, was indeed but the exquisite fragment of a once large and sumptuous villa. Two centuries of the play of the sea-wind were in the velvet of the mosses which lay along its inaccessible ledges and angles. Here and there the marble plates had slipped from their places, where the delicate weeds had forced their way. The graceful wildness which prevailed in garden and farm gave place to a singular nicety about the actual habitation, and a still more scrupulous sweetness and order reigned within. The old Roman architects seem to have well understood the decorative value of the floor—the real economy there was, in the production of rich interior effect, of a somewhat lavish expenditure upon the surface they trod on. The pavement of the hall had lost something of its evenness; but, though a little rough to the foot, polished and cared for like a piece of silver, looked, as mosaic-work is apt to do, its best in old age. Most noticeable among the ancestral masks, each in its little cedarn chest below the cornice, was that of the wasteful but elegant Marcellus, with the quaint resemblance in its waxen features to Marius, just then so full of animation and country colour. A chamber, curved ingeniously into oval form, which he had added to the mansion, still contained his collection of works of art; above all, that head of Medusa, for which the villa was famous. The spoilers of one of the old Greek towns on the coast had flung away or lost the thing, as it seemed, in some rapid flight across the river below, from the sands of which it was drawn up in a fisherman's net, with the fine golden *laminae* still clinging here and there to the bronze. It was Marcellus also who had contrived the prospect-tower of two storeys with the white pigeon-house above, so characteristic of the place. The little glazed windows in the uppermost chamber framed each its dainty landscape—the pallid crags of Carrara, like wildly twisted snow-drifts above the purple heath; the distant harbour with its freight of white marble going to sea; the lighthouse temple of *Venus Speciosa* on its dark headland, amid the long-drawn curves of white breakers. Even on summer nights the air there had always a motion in it, and drove the scent of new mown hay along all the passages of the house.

WALTER PATER *Marius the Epicurean*

2

Continue the examination of the imagery of the Joyce text (*p* 50), paying attention to progressions and contrasts in *sound* and *colour* images.

By means of a close examination of the images try to account for the strong sense of movement conveyed–'the rise and fall' of the passage.

Show how the sense-impressions of space and movement–of height and of depth, and of rise and fall–embody the emotional tones of the text.

3

[A]

A silent, dim, distanceless, steaming, rotting day in March. The last brown oak-leaf which had stood out the winter's frost spun and quivered plump down, and then lay; as if ashamed to have broken for a moment the ghastly stillness, like an awkward guest at a great dumb dinner-party. A cold suck of wind just proved its existence, by toothaches on the north side of all faces. The spiders, having been weather-bewitched the night before, had unanimously agreed to cover every brake and briar with gossamer-cradles, and never a fly to be caught in them; like Manchester cotton-spinners madly glutting the markets in the teeth of 'no demand'. The steam crawled out of the dank turf, and reeled off the flanks and nostrils of the shivering horses, and clung with clammy paws to frosted hats and dripping boughs. A soulless, skyless, catarrhal day, as if that bustling dowager, old mother Earth–what with match-making in spring, and *fêtes champêtres* in summer, and dinner-giving in autumn– was fairly worn out, and put to bed with the influenza, under wet blankets and the cold-water cure.

CHARLES KINGSLEY Yeast

[B]

At the same time, he hugged his shuddering body in both his arms–clasping himself, as if to hold himself together–and limped towards the low church wall. As I saw him go, picking his way among the nettles, and among the brambles that bound the green mounds, he looked in my young eyes as if he were eluding the hands of the dead people, stretching up cautiously out of their graves, to get a twist upon his ankle and pull him in.

When he came to the low church wall, he got over it, like a man whose legs were numbed and stiff, and then turned round to look for me. When I saw him turning, I set my face towards home, and made the best use of my legs. But presently I looked over my shoulder, and saw him going on again towards the river, still hugging himself in both arms, and picking his way with his sore feet among the great stones dropped into the marshes here and there, for stepping-places when the rains were heavy, or the tide was in.

The marshes were just a long black horizontal line then, as I stopped to look after him; and the river was just another horizontal line, not nearly so broad nor yet so black; and the sky was just a row of long angry red lines and dense black lines intermixed. On the edge of the river I could faintly make out the only two black things in all that prospect that seemed to be standing upright: one of these was the beacon by which the sailors steered—like an unhooped cask upon a pole—an ugly thing when you were near it; the other, a gibbet with some chains hanging to it which had once held a pirate. The man was limping on towards this latter, as if he were the pirate come to life, and come down, and going back to hook himself up again. It gave me a terrible turn when I thought so; and, as I saw the cattle lifting their heads to gaze after him, I wondered whether they thought so too.

CHARLES DICKENS *Great Expectations*

1 Collect sufficient examples of linked images from each of the above texts to support a considered statement of the effect aimed at by each writer.
2 Consider critically the effectiveness of the three sustained similes in Passage A.

3 Comment closely on the varying methods employed by Dickens in each of the three paragraphs in Passage B. (The commentaries on pages 45 and 49 may serve as a guide.)

4

[A]

The frost held for many weeks, until the birds were dying rapidly. Everywhere in the fields and under the hedges lay the ragged remains of lapwings, starlings, thrushes, redwings, innumerable ragged bloody cloaks of birds, when the flesh was eaten by invisible beasts of prey.

Then, quite suddenly, one morning, the change came. The wind went to the south, came off the sea warm and soothing. In the afternoon there were little gleams of sunshine, and the doves began, without interval, slowly and awkwardly to coo. The doves were cooing, though with a laboured sound, as if they were still winter-stunned. Nevertheless, all the afternoon they continued their noise, in the mild air, before the forst had thawed off the road. At evening the wind blew gently, still gathering a bruising quality of frost from the hard earth. Then, in the yellow-gleamy sunset, wild birds began to whistle faintly in the blackthorn thickets of the stream-bottom.

It was startling and almost frightening after the heavy silence of frost. How could they sing at once, when the ground was thickly strewn with the torn carcasses of birds? Yet out of the evening came the uncertain, silvery sounds that made one's soul stand alert, almost with fear. How could the little silver bugles sound the rally so swiftly, in the soft air, when the earth was yet bound? Yet the birds continued their whistling, rather dimly and brokenly, but throwing the threads of silver, germinating noise into the air.

D. H. LAWRENCE *Whistling of Birds* [from *Phoenix*]

[B]

The green paths down the hillsides are channels for streams. The young wheat is streaked by silver lines of water running

59

between the ridges, the sheep are gathered together on the slopes. After the wet dark days, the country seems more populous. It peoples itself in the sunbeams. The garden, mimic of spring, is gay with flowers. The purple-starred hepatica spreads itself in the sun, and the clustering snow-drops put forth their white heads, at first upright, ribbed with green, and like a rosebud when completely opened, hanging their heads downwards, but slowly lengthening their slender stems. The slanting woods of an unvarying brown, showing the light through the thin net-work of their upper boughs. Upon the highest ridge of that round hill covered with planted oaks, the shafts of the trees show in the light like the columns of a ruin.

DOROTHY WORDSWORTH *Journal*

[C]

But turn out of the way a little, good Scholar, towards yonder high honeysuckle hedge; there we'll sit and sing whilst this shower falls so gently upon the teeming earth, and gives yet a sweeter smell to the lovely flowers that adorn these verdant Meadows.

Look, under that broad beech tree, I sat down, when I was last this way a fishing, and the birds in the adjoining grove seemed to have a friendly contention with an Echo, whose dead voice seemed to live in a hollow tree, near to the brow of that Primrose-hill; there I sat viewing the silver-streams glide silently towards their centre, the tempestuous sea; yet, sometimes opposed by rugged roots, and pebble stones, which broke their waves, and turned them into foam: and sometimes I beguiled time by viewing the harmless lambs, some leaping securely in the cool shade, whilst others sported themselves in the cheerful sun: and saw others craving comfort from the swollen udders of their bleating dams. As thus I sat, these and other sights had so fully possessed my soul with content, that I thought as the Poet has happily ex-pressed it:

I was for that time lifted above earth;
And possessed joys not promised in my birth.

ISAAK WALTON The Compleat Angler

1 Compare the image sources employed in those passages. Which text contrasts sharply with the others in this respect? Support your answer with a selection of the available evidence.
2 What image features can you find that are common to all three passages? Consider content, tone and purpose when answering the question.
3 Basing your answer chiefly on the images – but using any other significant evidence – describe the emotional tones of each passage.

5

Consider the imagery of the following passages in the light of the observations on the nature and function of imagery made in Section 7. (You must, of course, establish sense, tone, and intention, and decide what kind of writing each is before a critical approach to the use of imagery is possible.) Note, too, the chief features of the diction and comment on the structure and movement where relevant.

[A]

Neither must we think that the life of a man begins when he can feed himself, or walk alone, when he can fight or beget his like; for so he is contemporary with a camel or a cow: but he is first a man, when he comes to a certain steady use of reason, according to his proportion; and when that is, all the world of men cannot tell precisely. Some are called *at age* at fourteen, some at one-and-twenty, some never; but all men late enough, for the life of a man comes upon him slowly and insensibly. But as when the sun approaches towards the gates of the morning, he first opens a little eye of heaven, and sends away the spirits of darkness, and gives light to a cock, and calls up the lark to matins, and by and by gilds the fringes of a cloud, and peeps over the eastern hills, thrusting out his golden horns, like those which decked the brows of *Moses* when he was forced to wear a veil, because himself had seen the face of God; and still while a man tells the story, the sun gets up higher, till he shews a fair face and a full light, and then he shines one whole day, under a cloud often, and sometimes weeping great and little showers, and sets quickly: so is a man's reason and his life.

JEREMY TAYLOR *Holy Dying*

[B]

And it is just the same with men's best wisdom. When you come to a good book, you must ask yourself, 'Am I inclined to work as an Australian miner would? Are my pickaxes and shovels in good order, and am I in good trim myself, my sleeves well up to the elbow, and my breath good, and my temper?' And, keeping the figure a little longer, even at cost of tiresomeness, for it is a thoroughly useful one, the metal you are in search of being the author's mind or meaning, his words are as the rock which you have to crush and smelt in order to get at it. And your pickaxes are your own care, wit, and learning; your smelting furnace is your own thoughtful soul. Do not hope to get at any good author's meaning without those tools and that fire; often you will need sharpest, finest chiselling, and patientist fusing, before you can gather one grain of the metal.

JOHN RUSKIN *Sesame and Lilies*

[C]

Ought not winter, in allegorical designs, the rather to be represented with such things that might suggest hope than such as convey a cold and grim despair? The withered leaf, the snowflake, the hedging bill that cuts and destroys, why these? Why not rather the dear larks for one? They fly in flocks, and amid the white expanse of snow (in the south) their pleasant twitter or call is heard as they sweep along seeking for some grassy spot cleared by the wind. The lark, the bird of the light, is there in the bitter short days. Put the lark then for winter, a sign of hope, a certainty of summer. Put, too, the sheathed bud, for if you search the hedge you will find the buds there, on tree and bush, carefully wrapped around with the case which protects them as a cloak. Put, too, the sharp needles of the green corn; let the wind clear it of snow a little way, and show that under cold clod and colder snow the green thing pushes up, knowing that summer must come. Nothing despairs but man. Set the sharp curve of the white new moon in the sky: she is white in true frost, and yellow a little if it is devising change. Set the new moon as something that symbols an increase. Set the shepherd's crook in a corner as a token that the flocks are already en-larged in number. The shepherd is the symbolic man of the hardest winter time. His work is never more important than then. Those that only roam the fields when they are pleasant in May, see the lambs at play in the meadow, and naturally think of lambs and May flowers. But the lamb was born in the adversity of snow. Or you might set the morning star, for it burns and glitters in the winter dawn and throws forth beams like those of metal consumed in oxygen. There is nought that I know by comparison with which I might indicate the glory of the morning star, while yet the dark night hides in the hollows. The lamb is born in the fold. The morning star glitters in the sky. The bud is alive in its sheath; the green corn under the snow; the lark twitters as he passes. Now these to me are the allegory of winter.

RICHARD JEFFERIES The Open Air

[D]

But it was Tom King's face that advertised him unmistakably for what he was. It was the face of a typical prize fighter; of one who had put in long years of service in the squared ring, and, by that means, developed and emphasised all the marks of the fighting beast. It was distinctly a lowering countenance, and, that no feature of it might escape notice, it was clean-shaven. The lips were shapeless and constituted a mouth harsh to excess, that was like a gash in his face. The jaw was aggressive, brutal, heavy. The eyes, slow of movement and heavy-lidded, were almost expressionless under the shaggy, indrawn brows. Sheer animal that he was, the eyes were the most animal-like feature about him. They were sleepy, lion-like – the eyes of a fighting animal. The forehead slanted quickly back to the hair, which, clipped close, showed every bump of a villainous-looking head. A nose twice broken and moulded variously by countless blows, and a cauliflower ear, permanently swollen and distorted to twice its size, completed his adornment, while the beard, fresh-shaven as it was, sprouted in the skin and gave the face a blue-black stain.

Altogether, it was the face of a man to be afraid of in a dark alley or lonely place. And yet Tom King was not a criminal, nor had he ever done anything criminal. Outside of brawls, common to his walk in life, he had harmed no one. Nor had he ever been know to pick a quarrel. He was a professional, and all the fighting brutishness of him was reserved for his professional appearances. Outside the ring he was slow-going, easy-natured, and, in his younger days, when money was flush, too open-handed for his own good. He bore no grudges and had few enemies. Fighting was a business with him. In the ring he struck to hurt, struck to maim, struck to destroy; but there was no animus in it. It was a plain business proposition. Audiences assembled and paid for the spectacle of two men knocking each other out. The winner took the big end of the purse. When Tom King faced the Woolloomoolloo Gouger, twenty years before, he knew that the Gouger's jaw was only four months healed after having been broken in a Newcastle bout. And he had played for that jaw and broken it again in the ninth round, not because he bore the Gouger any ill will, but because that was the surest way to put the Gouger out and win the big end of the purse. Nor had the Gouger borne him any ill will for it. It was the game, and both knew the game and played it.

Tom King had never been a talker, and he sat by the window, morosely silent, staring at his hands. The veins stood out on the backs of the hands, large and swollen; and the knuckles, smashed and battered and malformed, testified to the use to which they had been put. He had never heard that a man's life was the life of his arteries, but well he knew the meaning of those big, upstanding veins. His heart had pumped too much blood through them at top pressure. They no longer did the work. He had stretched the elasticity out of them, and with their distension had passed his endurance. He tired easily now. No longer could he do a fast twenty rounds, hammer and tongs, fight, fight, fight, from gong to gong, with fierce rally on top of fierce rally, beaten to the ropes and in turn beating his opponent to the ropes, and rallying fiercest and fastest of all in that last, twentieth round, with the house on its feet and yelling, himself rushing, striking, ducking, raining showers of blows upon showers of blows and receiving showers of blows in return, and all the time the heart faithfully pumping the surging blood through the adequate veins. The veins, swollen at the time, had always shrunk down again, though not quite–each time, imperceptibly at first, remaining just a trifle larger than before. He stared at them and at his battered knuckles, and, for the moment, caught a vision of the youthful excellence of those hands before the first knuckle had been smashed on the head of Benny Jones, otherwise known as the Welsh Terror.

JACK LONDON *A Piece of Steak*

8
Prose rhythms

A great deal has been written on the subject of prose rhythms, and in this section an attempt is made to present the basic information necessary for further study. What follows should, therefore, be regarded as a series of useful hints, providing a sound foundation on which the critic can build.

The word *prose* itself affords a starting point for the discussion. Its literal meaning is 'straightforward discourse' and it is defined in the *Oxford English Dictionary* thus: 'The ordinary form of written or spoken language, without metrical structure.' The definition is reminiscent of Aristotle's description of prose as 'neither possessing metre nor destitute of rhythm.' Yet, of course, the *elements* of metre are present in prose; for prose, like verse, is made of words.* The difference lies in the fact that prose submerges its metrical elements, whereas in verse they are exhibited. Fuller discussion of metre will be found later in the section.

But, as will have become clear in earlier sections of this book, we cannot meaningfully talk of 'prose' as if there were only one kind. We can talk of 'prose' to distinguish it from 'verse'; but we have to recognise that there are different kinds of prose fitted for different tasks. And as there is a theoretically infinite linguistic range from which a particular writer will make a particular selection to perform a particular task, so he will exploit the rhythmic resources of language to achieve desired effects, ranging from the highly rhythmic to the a-rhythmic, according to his purposes—and, of course, his skill. The following quotation summarises the critical approach advocated: an approach applied successively to diction and imagery, and now to prose rhythms:

[The study of style] treats of the selection among linguistic

*' . . . for próse, like vérse, is máde of wórds.'

responses possible in a given situation. It shows how one man will use certain words and syntactical constructions whereas another man will employ a more or less different linguistic medium. It also shows that different situations call for different words and phrases, quite aside from the obvious requirements of meaning.

EDGAR H. STURTEVANT *An Introduction to Linguistic Science*

For a particular task, the writer chooses particular rhythms which–analysed by the critic–are seen as an integral part of the style; powerful in affective language, muted in expository prose. When dealing with rhythm, as when dealing with diction and imagery, the critic necessarily focuses his attention on detail and isolates one element of style from the rest. Such dissection is a preliminary to the appreciation of the whole. The surgeon is skilled in anatomy, yet his care is for the living body. The synthesis undertaken in the final stage of criticism (see Sections 5 and 9) restores perspective. We study the elements of style the better to appreciate the style itself: we study the style itself the better to appreciate the whole, which is at once matter *and* manner– *what* is said, and *how* it is said.

'Flux and reflux, swell and cadence, that is the movement for a sentence.' De Quincey's words are a useful introduction to a consideration of prose rhythms.

Language has two modes: spoken and written. Spoken language is a series of sounds which symbolise 'meanings'. Written language is a series of letters which symbolise sounds which themselves symbolise 'meanings'. Written language comes to the reader through both the eye and the ear (you 'hear' what you are reading even though you are reading silently), the eye being prime, but the ear playing a considerable part.

The act of composing in prose may be considered under three headings. It is not suggested that the operations about to be described are carried out in the sequence here adopted; nor is it intended to suggest that each is a conscious process. The degree of *conscious* intention will vary. Much that is written will flow with the effortlessness born of ability and experience; but the critic will profitably apply an analytical approach to what may be unconsciously achieved. And it is certain that the prose writer checked in his flow or disappointed with an effect will then consciously pursue the activities now listed:

1 Selection of the words required to communicate the ideas, thoughts and feelings that are the 'content' of the passage.
2 Arrangement – ordering – of the 'lexical' elements according to the syntax of the language in order to communicate at all.
3 Selection of 'artistic' devices to achieve greater force and clarity and to make the prose attractive.

When considering diction and imagery, some attention was paid to 1. This present inquiry into rhythm concentrates on 2 and 3 and their interaction.

The main elements constituting prose rhythms may be represented by the following diagrams:

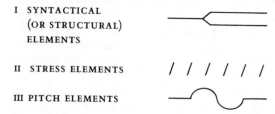

I SYNTACTICAL
(OR STRUCTURAL)
ELEMENTS

II STRESS ELEMENTS

III PITCH ELEMENTS

Each will now be considered in turn.

I SYNTACTICAL (OR STRUCTURAL) ELEMENTS
The commonest rhythmical device is *parallelism*, usually syntactical, but capable of operating at any of the levels into which, for present purposes, written texts can be divided. These levels form a hierarchy:

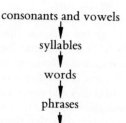

consonants and vowels
↓
syllables
↓
words
↓
phrases
↓

clauses

↓

sentences

↓

paragraphs

For example, the devices of alliteration and assonance – often, but not always, accompanying parallel syntactical constructions – depend for their effect on parallelism of sound.

Wanton jests make fools laugh, and wise men frown.

Seeing we are civilised Englishmen, let us not be naked savages in our talk. Such rotten speeches are worst in withered age, when men run after that sin in their words which flieth from them in the deed.

It is impossible to isolate the purely phonological (sound) effects even in such simple examples as those; for they are part of a complex of lexical, syntactical and stress devices, reminding us of the power of parallelism which, at varied linguistic levels, sets up a rhythm of sound and echo and interweaves 'phonology' and 'meaning'. The device of repetition – whatever form it takes, and whether simple repetition or repetition 'with a difference' – is a powerful weapon in the armoury of prose, which necessarily – and by definition – lacks the formalised patterns of verse.

To achieve memorability and 'punch', simple repetition of letters and/or of words is frequently employed in everyday sayings, aphorisms, and proverbs:

It is good grafting on a good stock.

Great almsgiving lessens no man's living.

Haste makes waste, and waste makes want, and want makes strife between the goodman and his wife.

Sometimes the same qualities are sought by the juxtapositioning of opposites:

Great boast and small roast.

Old sin makes new shame.

Laugh before breakfast and you'll cry before supper.

But syntactical parallelism (often combined with phonological, stress, and pitch elements) achieves a more subtle rhythmic effect: sound and sense, content and 'audible shape', then interact:

There was ever more in him to be praised than to be pardoned.

BEN JONSON

Man is a noble animal, splendid in ashes and pompous in the grave.

SIR THOMAS BROWNE

The critic can often make the audible shape visible by adopting some graphic method of presentation:

There was ever more in him   to be praised   than
                              to be pardoned.

Man is a noble animal,   splendid in ashes   and
                              pompous in the grave

The syntactical rhythms of the Authorised Version of the Bible— more often talked about than analysed—stand out clearly if graphically presented:

The wilderness and the solitary place shall be glad for them:
   and the desert shall rejoice and blossom as the rose.
It shall blossom abundantly,
   and rejoice even with joy and singing:
The glory of Lebanon shall be given unto it,
   the excellency of Carmel and Sharon:
They shall see the glory of the Lord,
   and the excellency of our God.

From ISAIAH 35

As was stressed in Section 4, the particular methods of analysis

applied to the examples given in this book are intended as suggestions only. Each critic must find his own techniques and select
from them as seems appropriate in each case; but at least he has a
starting point if he lays bare the syntactical 'skeleton', as was done
with the *Isaiah* passage above and as will now be done with the
examples that follow.

For it is one thing to be eloquent in the Schools,
   or in the Hall;
another at the Bar,
   or in the Pulpit.
There is a difference between Mooting and Pleading;
   between Fencing and Fighting.

BEN JONSON Discoveries

```
For their    sight    in civil regiment is but
                                              blindness,
             strength
      their
                    weakness,
             counsel
      their
                    foolishness,
             judgement
      and
                    frenzy,
         if it be rightly considered.
```

JOHN KNOX Regiment of Women

```
        ⟋ (i) not to contradict and confute,  ⟍
Read  ─  (ii) nor to believe and take for granted,  ═ but ➤
        ⟍ (iii) nor to find talk and discourse,  ⟋                ⟍
  ⟍_____⟋
      ➤ to weigh and consider.
```

FRANCIS BACON Of Studies [in Essays]

Note that a graphical presentation not only lays bare the
structure of a text, but may also highlight the critical significance
of lexical items. The diagrammatic treatment of the Knox passage

emphasises the thumping antitheses (strength/weakness, etc.) and so helps to account for the bullying tone. The firm control of an intricate structure in the Bacon passage reinforces the 'meaning' (the control and the structure are, of course, part of the 'meaning') and both convey the coolness of consideration.

Another device by means of which the *overall* structure of a passage may be made clear can be demonstrated by a consideration of two sustained and rather difficult passages.

[A]

But the Quincunx of Heaven runs low, and 'tis time to close the five ports of knowledge; We are unwilling to spin out our awakening thoughts into phantasmes of sleep, which often continueth praecognitions; making Cables of Cobwebbes, and Wildernesses of handsome Groves. Beside *Hippocrates* hath spoke so little, and the Oneirocriticall Masters have left such frigid Interpretations from Plants, that there is little encouragement to dream of Paradise itself. Nor will the sweetest delight in Gardens afford much comfort in sleep: wherein the dulnesse of that sense shakes hands with delectable odours: and though in the bed of *Cleopatra* can hardly with any delight raise up the ghost of a Rose.

Night, which Pagan Theology could make the daughter of Chaos, affords no advantage to the description of order: Although no lower than that Masse can we derive its Genealogy. All things began in order, so shall they end, and so shall they begin again; according to the ordainer of order and mystical Mathematicks of the City of Heaven.

Though *Somnus* in *Homer* be sent to rowse up *Agamemnon*, I finde no such effects in these drowsy approaches of sleep. To keep our eyes open longer were but to act our *Antipodes*. The Huntsmen are up in *America*, and they are already past their first sleep in *Persia*. But who can be drowsie at that howr which freed us from everlasting sleep? or have slumbering thoughts at that time, when sleep itself must end, and as some conjecture all shall awake again?

SIR THOMAS BROWNE *The Garden of Cyrus*

[B]

Now I saw in my Dream, that by this time the Pilgrims were got over the Inchanted Ground, and entering in the Country of *Beulah*, whose Air was very sweet and pleasant, the way lying directly through it, they solaced themselves there for a season. Yea, here they heard continually the singing of Birds, and saw every day the flowers appear in the earth; and heard the voice of the Turtle in the Land. In this Country the Sun shineth night and day; wherefore this was beyond the Valley of the *Shadow* of *Death*, and also out of reach of *Giant Despair*; neither could they from this place so much as see *Doubting-Castle*. Here they were within sight of the City they were going to: also here met them some of the Inhabitants thereof; For in this Land the Shining Ones commonly walked, because it was on the borders of Heaven. In this Land also the contract between the Bride and the Bridegroom was renewed; Yea here, *as the Bridegroom rejoyceth over the Bride, so did their God rejoyce over them.* Here they had no want of Corn and Wine; for in this place they met with abundance of what they had sought for in all their Pilgrimages. Here they heard voices from out of the City, loud voices, saying, *Say ye to the daughter of Zion, Behold thy salvation cometh; behold, his reward is with him.* Here all the Inhabitants of the Country called them, *The holy people, the redeemed of the Lord, sought out.*

JOHN BUNYAN *The Pilgrim's Progress*

Take semi-colons, colons, and full-stops as marking the end of 'lines' in the above passages and use a capital X to represent each word, ten Xs to a group. The following 'shapes' then emerge:

[A]
```
XXXXXXXXXX  XXXXXXX
XXXXXXXXXX  XXXXXXXX
XXXXXXXXXX
XXXXXXXXXX  XXXXXXXXXX  XXXXXXX
XXXXXXXXXX  XX
XXXXXXXXXX  X
XXXXXXXXXX  XXXXXXXXX
```

```
XXXXXXXXXX   XXXXXXXX
XXXXXXXXXX   X
XXXXXXXXXX   XXXXX
XXXXXXXXXX   XXXX

XXXXXXXXXX   XXXXXXXXXX  X
XXXXXXXXXX   XX
XXXXXXXXXX   XXXXXX
XXXXXXXXXX   XXXX
XXXXXXXXXX   XXXXXXXXXX
```

[B]
```
XXXXXXXXXX   XXXXXXXXXX  XXXXXXXXXX
             XXXXXXXXXX  XXXXX
XXXXXXXXXX   XXXXXXXXX
XXXXXXXXXX
XXXXXXXXX
XXXXXXXXXX   XXXXXXXXX
XXXXXXXXXX   XX
XXXXXXXXXX   XX
XXXXXXXXX
XXXXXXXXXX   XXXXXXX
XXXXXXXXXX   XXXX
XXXXXXXXXX   XXXXXX
XXXXXXXXX
XXXXXXXXXX   XXXXXXX
XXXXXXXXXX   XXXXXXXXXX  XXX
XXXXXX
XXXXXXXXXX   XXXXXXXXX
```

As the diagrams show, the two passages split into exactly 16 'lines'
each. Browne's line groups show up as more tightly controlled
than Bunyan's, resulting in a more compact 'audible shape'. The
paragraphing in Passage A also contributes to the same effect,
giving a 'stanzaic' structure. But more remarkable is the much
greater disparity in length between Bunyan's longest 'line' and his
shortest, as compared with Browne's. In Passage B the ratio between the longest and the shortest line is $7\frac{1}{2}$:1. In Passage A the
ratio is 3:1. It is not suggested that so detailed a pictorial analysis of

shape is necessary to a just criticism of every prose text; or, indeed, that the method adopted above is the only one or the best one. But it is a way of making apparent different structures, which must then be assessed in relation to tone and intention, to other rhythmic elements, and to diction and imagery. In the above passages, for example, the tightness of Browne's structure and the looseness of Bunyan's are paralleled by the clustered stresses of the former and the diffused stresses of the latter. Again, the image sources of Browne are quite different from Bunyan's.

Now attempt FOR PRACTICE I on page 82.

The texts just studied in FOR PRACTICE I, and the examples furnished in the section, provide illustrations of the use of parallelism at each of the linguistic levels described on p. 68. Any pattern of repetition, whether structural, phonological, or accentual, should be noticed by the critic and, where possible, interpreted. It is improbable that such patterns are fortuitous, for within the comparatively loose overall structure of prose (loose when compared with verse structures, that is) a stylistic signal of this kind is almost certainly both a pointer to, and a means of expressing, sense, tone, and purpose.

Some of the most famous examples of prose patterning occur in Sir Thomas Browne's *Urn Burial*. An extract from this work will help to reinforce the points just made.

And therefore restless inquietude for the diuturnity of our memories unto present considerations, seems a vanity almost out of date, and superannuated piece of folly. We cannot hope to live so long in our names, as some have done in their persons; one face of Janus holds no proportion unto the other. 'Tis too late to be ambitious. The great mutations of the world are acted, or time may be too short for our designs. To extend our memories by Monuments, whose death we daily pray for, and whose duration we cannot hope, without injury to our expectations, in the advent of the last day, were a contradiction to our beliefs. We whose generations are ordained in this setting part of time, are providentially taken off from such imaginations. And being necessitated to eye the remaining particle of futurity, are naturally constituted unto thoughts of the next world, and cannot excusably decline the consideration of that duration, which maketh Pyramids pillars of snow, and all that's past a moment.

The critic will often find that close attention to sentence patterns provides him with his first insight into structural or syntactical rhythms, and his interpretation of the evidence afforded by graphic 'plots' may be made more fruitful by considering the selected and plotted sentences under these headings (there is, of course, overlap between the two main headings):

Grammatical classification:
simple sentence;
compound sentence;
complex sentence.
Stylistic classification:
loose sentence;
periodic sentence;
balanced sentence.

Mere classification is not, of course, the aim. Nor is a purely sentence-based analysis sufficient. There is no single critical way–no golden road–but experience shows that such an approach can lead to recognition of basic patterns which, when grasped, may provide an appreciation of the texture of the writing as a whole.

The earlier writers of English prose were content with the more obvious rhythmic effects: with recognisable repetitions of parallel constructions. By the end of the Elizabethan period more subtle forms of syntactical rhythms were practised: long and sustained undulations produced by varied arrangements of compound-complex sentences. This general method–adapted in innumerable ways to the varying needs and purposes of individual writers–held good until the last decade or so of the nineteenth century.

The twentieth century writer, on the other hand, seems to rely less on syntactical repetitions and more on an interplay between a *primary* rhythm (marked by the grammatical units–phrases, clauses, sentences) and a *secondary* rhythm (marked by stress groups, but *not* regular and, therefore, not metrical). Some writers call the primary rhythm *thought-rhythm* (because it is syntax-based) and the secondary rhythm *sound-rhythm* (because it is stress-based). Of course, the two rhythms can never be separated. The critic may notice the coincidence or the counterpointing of one with or against the other, but they overlap and interact continually. Indeed, neither can exist without the other; for it is only by the presence of one that we can recognise the presence of the other.

The following passage from D. H. Lawrence illustrates the point and its rhythms may be compared with those of the text from *Urn Burial*.

So the change, the endless and rapid change. In the sunny countries, the change seems more vivid, and more complete than in the grey countries. In the grey countries, there is a grey or dark permanency, over whose surface passes change ephemeral, leaving no real mark. In England, winters and summers shadowily give place to one another. But underneath lies the grey substratum, the permanency of cold, dark reality where bulbs live, and reality is bulbous, a thing of endurance and stored-up, starchy energy.

But in the sunny countries, change is the reality and permanence is artificial and a condition of imprisonment. In the North, man tends instinctively to imagine, to conceive that the sun is lighted like a candle, in an everlasting darkness, and that one day the candle will go out, the sun will be exhausted, and the everlasting dark will resume uninterrupted sway. Hence, to the northerner, the temporal world is essentially tragical, because it is temporal and must cease to exist, and this is the root of the feeling of tragedy.

But to the southerner, the sun is so dominant that, if every phenomenal body disappeared out of the universe, nothing would remain but bright luminousness, sunniness. The absolute is sunniness; and shadow, or dark, is only merely

relative: merely the result of something getting between one`
and the sun.

D. H. LAWRENCE *Flowery Tuscany*
[from *Phoenix*]

The parallelism of construction, recognisably repeated, that was
for so long the dominant feature of English prose rhythms is not
much in evidence there. The other elements of rhythm, to which
we now turn, were present, of course, long before the twentieth
century, but commonly in conjunction with, and subordinate in
effect to, syntactical rhythms. Now, a more dominant role seems
to have been assigned to these other rhythmic elements.

II STRESS ELEMENTS

Metre is a more or less regular *pattern* of stressed and unstressed
('slack') syllables. The stressed and slack syllables, so grouped into
patterns, form the various kinds of 'feet' known to English
scansion. (There are four basic feet in English metres: the *iamb* x ∕;
the *trochee* ∕ x; the *anapaest* x x ∕; the *dactyl* ∕ x x). As we have
seen, the presence of metre is the distinguishing quality of *verse*;
the absence of metre is the distinguishing quality of *prose*. Yet, as
we have also seen, prose–because it is made of words–contains
the elements of metre, for syllabic stress is an inherent feature
of the English Language. It is, moreover, a particularly strong
feature, because the English Language, having so few inflexions,
depends greatly upon word order for its syntax. To use the stock
example, in the two sentences 'The dog bit John.' and 'John bit
the dog.' it is word order that tells us which is the subject and
which is the object. The words themselves do not change to
signal 'case' (as they would in, say, Latin or German): it is word
order alone that does the trick. Because of this absence of grammatical inflexion, intonation and stress are particularly important,
for they reinforce the syntactical arrangement of the words.

Stress, then, inevitably occurs in prose, performing two main
functions: (*a*) an underlining, as it were, of the 'sense'; (*b*) a
reinforcement of the 'emotion'. It is obviously an aid to clear
communication if the most important words in a sentence are
stressed; and strong emotional content results in, and is expressed
by, a more than usual number of stressed syllables.

Since stress is such an important element in prose, it is neither surprising nor, necessarily, an occasion for critical tut-tutting when metrical runs appear. But, since it is of the very nature of prose to be a-metrical, the *obtrusion* of such runs is felt to be a weakness. Often, the run will be barely noticeable. To find it, the critic would have to read in such a way as to force the metrical stresses into prominence and so distort the normal speech stresses. But when the prose writer seeks deliberately for metrical effects, either as ornament or as an artificial heightening of emotion, then he is at fault. Strong and sustained metrical patterning being alien to the nature of prose, but native to the nature of verse, such patterning breaks down the organic structure of prose and creates a hybrid form, neither true prose nor true verse.

Let us look again at the De Quincey quotation already used to introduce the topic of prose rhythms:

Flux and reflux, swell and cadence, that is the movement for a sentence.

A graphic plot shows clearly why De Quincey structured the sentence as he did:

Flux	re	swell	cad	that	move	for
and	flux,	and	ence,	is the	ment	a
sent						
ence.						

It looks good: the parallel structures match the sense, and stresses reinforce the parallelism. But does it sound good?

／ X ／ X ／ X ／ X ／ X X ／ X ／ X
Flux and reflux, swell and cadence, that is the movement for a
／ X
sentence.

Who is right here – De Quincey, or the critic? Did De Quincey force this strong metrical effect? Or is the critic forcing it by insensitive, sing-song reading? Does the strength of the structure (lying in the harmony between the syntactical shape and the sense) silence the jingle of the alien feet? Does De Quincey's intention justify the metrical run? These are questions to be answered; and they are typical of the questions that constantly arise when the stress elements in prose rhythms are under consideration.

The strongest and most 'natural' metre in the English Language is the iambic. That disyllabic rising foot constantly lurks beneath the surface of prose, and frequently breaks through. George Saintsbury *(A History of English Prose Rhythm)* makes the point memorably: 'The beautiful bane of blank verse has been found repeatedly in all writers of formal prose.'

Here, as everywhere, the critic, having mastered the basic knowledge of the nature of prose and verse structures and the effects proper to each medium, must, finally, trust to his own judgment and taste. General principles may be offered for general guidance—for example, Helen Griffith's statement: 'Flowing line, rather than recurrent pattern, is the characteristic of good fluid prose . . .' *(Time Patterns in Prose*, Princeton, 1929). But general statements are of general use only, and may need modification in particular cases. If the writer flouts the 'rules' and gets away with it, the critic may happily throw away his rule book and rejoice in the writer's achievement.

That being said, metre *is* a dangerous intruder into the territory of prose. Stresses naturally mark the centres of interest in sentences and may well occur in rhythmic repetitions; but the formalised patterns of metre are quite another thing. Like the ghost in *Hamlet*, metre in prose is an 'extravagant and erring spirit'.

Bearing in mind these points about stress, attempt FOR PRACTICE 2 on page 85.

III PITCH ELEMENTS

Prose rhythm, we have said, is based on three main elements: (I) parallelism of structure (sometimes syntactical, i.e. patterning of phrases, clauses, sentences: sometimes lexical, i.e. patterning of individual words); (II) stress patterns; (III) pitch patterns. This third element—pitch—is in many ways the most difficult to describe, yet in reading we are immediately and vividly conscious of its importance.

It is obvious that pitch is intimately bound up with 'meaning'. Of no element in prose style is it more important to emphasise that *what* we say affects *how* we say it: *how* we say it is part of *what* we say. As a very simple illustration, consider the sentence: 'That's a remarkable statement to make.' How we say it makes a profound difference to what we are saying. It is not only a question of stress— experiment by bringing the main stress down on different words and note the changes thus effected in the 'meaning'. It is also a matter of intonation; and, again, the point is readily illustrated by different readings. Consider, too, the effect on 'meaning' of changing 'That's . . .' into 'That is . . .' or by ending the sentence with an exclamation mark.

As in earlier sections, it is to be stressed that the isolation of individual stylistic elements for detailed examination is a deliberately artificial device. Here, we concentrate on pitch only to produce a clearer understanding of its operation in conjunction with the other elements of style.

Nor can the contribution of pitch to rhythm be fully exemplified in the study of single sentences. It is the *recurrence* of rise and fall in matching curves that sets up a discernible pitch rhythm. One sentence is but a unit – a curve, if you like; and perhaps itself composed of successive segments making up the unit curve of the individual sentence. But a *succession* of *corresponding* curves sets up those 'melodic waves' that play so powerful a part in establishing and communicating 'meaning' and 'emotion' and – together with structural and stress patterns – produce that fusion between the two which constitutes the total impact of a prose passage.

Pitch and stress are clearly related, and it is unlikely that even at this deliberately analytical stage of our examination we can profitably isolate one from the other. For example, *cadence* – one of the most commonly-employed rhythmic devices – when looked at in one way is the *fall* of a pitch curve. When looked at in another way it is part of a stress pattern. It is, in fact, best considered in both lights.

But yet she carried nothing with her wherein she trusted more than in herself, and in the charms and enchantment of her passing beauty and grace.

SIR THOMAS NORTH'S *Plutarch*

The whole sentence is based on syntactical parallelism, as a graphic plot would readily demonstrate. The second half – from *and* to *grace* – provides a striking example of the subtle interweaving of stress and pitch, and might be plotted thus:

In that plot the solid line represents the primary or thought-rhythm (syntax-based). The broken line represents the secondary or sound-rhythm (stress- and pitch-based). The curve reaches its height with the word *enchantment*; and at that point the 'arch' of the primary rhythm underpins the 'arch' of the secondary.

The syllabic cadence of:

$$\begin{array}{cccc} 3 & 2 & 1 & 1 \end{array}$$
her passing | beauty | and | grace

produces the characteristic 'dying fall' of an end-of-sentence cadence, and is reinforced by stress:

$$\longleftarrow / \longrightarrow \quad \longleftarrow / \rightarrow \qquad /$$
her passing beauty and grace

Note that, as so often in prose, stress here is not strictly syllabic. The stresses are frequently 'distributed': that is, they fall on *centres* of 'sense' and 'emotion', rather than on individual syllables.

FOR PRACTICE
1
Attempt a graphical analysis of each of the following texts, and state briefly the critical conclusions that can be drawn from each 'plot'.

[A]
The first Minister of State has not so much business in public as a wise man has in private; if the one have little leisure to be alone, the other has less leisure to be in company; the one has but part of the affairs of one Nation, the other all the works of God and Nature under his consideration. There is no saying shocks me so much as that which I hear very often, that a man does not know how to pass his time. 'Twould have been but ill-spoken by Methusalem in the nine hundred sixty-ninth year of his life; so far it is from us, who have not time enough to attain to the utmost perfection of any part of any Science, to have cause to complain that we are forced to be idle for want of work.

ABRAHAM COWLEY *Of Solitude* [in *Essays*]

[B]

Is not a Patron, my Lord, one who looks with unconcern upon a man struggling for life in the water, and, when he has reached ground, encumbers him with help? The notice that you have been pleased to take of my labours, had it been early, had it been kind; but it has been delayed till I am indifferent, and cannot enjoy it; till I am solitary, and cannot impart it; till I am known, and do not want it. I hope it is no very cynical asperity not to confess obligations where no benefit has been received, or to be unwilling that the public should consider me as owing that to a Patron, which Providence has enabled me to do for myself.

SAMUEL JOHNSON *Letter to Lord Chesterfield*

[C]

If it were not for the *Bible* and *Common Prayer Book* in the Vulgar Tongue, we should hardly be able to understand anything that was written among us an hundred years ago; which is certainly true: for those books, being perpetually read in Churches, have proved a kind of standard for language, especially to the common people. And I doubt whether the alterations since introduced have added much to the beauty or strength of the English Tongue, though they have taken off a great deal from that simplicity which is one of the greatest perfections in any language. You, my Lord, who are so conversant in the sacred writings, and so great a judge of them in their originals, will agree, that no translation our country ever yet produced, has come up to that of the *Old* and *New Testament*: And by the many beautiful passages which I have often had the honour to hear your Lordship cite from thence, I am persuaded that the translators of the *Bible* were masters of an English style much fitter for that work than any we see in our present writings; which I take to be owing to the simplicity that runs through the whole.

JONATHAN SWIFT *Letter Dedicatory to the Earl of Oxford*

[D]

This emperor Prester John, when he goes to battle against any other lord, has no banners borne before him; but he has three large crosses of gold full of precious stones; and each cross is set in a chariot full richly arrayed. And to keep each cross are appointed ten thousand men of arms, and more than one hundred thousand footmen. And this number of people is independent of the chief army. And when he has no war, but rides with a private company, he has before him but one plain cross of wood, in remembrance that Jesus Christ suffered death upon a wooden cross. And they carry before him also a platter of gold full of earth, in token that his nobleness, and his might, and his flesh, shall turn to earth. And he has borne before him also a vessel of silver, full of noble jewels of gold and precious stones, in token of his lordship, nobility, and power. He dwells commonly in the city of Susa, and there is his principal palace, which is so rich and noble that no man can conceive it without seeing it.

SIR JOHN MANDEVILLE *Travels*

[E]

The highest proof of virtue is to possess boundless power without abusing it. No kind of power is more formidable than the power of making men ridiculous; and that power Addison possessed in boundless measure. How grossly that power was abused by Swift and by Voltaire is well known. But of Addison it may be confidently affirmed that he has blackened no man's character, nay, that it would be difficult, if not impossible, to find in all the volumes which he has left us a single taunt which can be called ungenerous or unkind. Yet he had detractors, whose malignity might have seemed to justify as terrible a revenge as that which men, not superior to him in genius, wreaked on Bettesworth and on Franc de Pompignan. He was a politician; he was the best writer of his party; he lived in times of fierce excitement, in times when persons of high character and station stooped to scurrility such as is now practised only by the basest of mankind. Yet no provocation and no example could induce him to return railing for railing.

THOMAS BABINGTON MACAULAY *Essay on Addison*

2

Discuss the stress elements in the rhythm of these passages, distinguishing between the 'proper' use of rhythmic repetitions of stress and the 'obtrusion' of metrical runs. Use graphic plots whenever these are helpful, and note examples of the interplay of content, emotion, syntactical structure and stress. (You will, of course, decide on sense, tone, and intention before tackling the rhythms.) The longer passages can be taken a paragraph at a time.

[A]

At length there was a cry of silence, and a breathless look from all towards the door. The jury returned, and passed him close. He could glean nothing from their faces; they might as well have been of stone. Perfect stillness ensured – not a rustle – not a breath – Guilty.

The building rang with a tremendous shout, and another, and another, and then it echoed loud groans, then gathered strength as they swelled out, like angry thunder. It was a peal of joy from the populace outside, greeting the news that he would die on Monday.

The noise subsided, and he was asked if he had anything to say why sentence of death should not be passed upon him. He had resumed his listening attitude, and looked intently at his questioner while the demand was made; but it was twice repeated before he seemed to hear it, and then he only muttered that he was an old man – an old man – an old man – and so, dropping into a whisper, was silent again.

The judge assumed the black cap, and the prisoner still stood with the same air and gesture. A woman in the gallery uttered some exclamation called forth by this dread solemnity; he looked hastily up as if angry at the interruption, and bent forward yet more attentively. The address was solemn and impressive; the sentence fearful to hear. But he stood, like a marble figure, without the motion of a nerve. His haggard face was still thrust forward, his underjaw hanging down, and his eyes staring out before him, when the jailer put his hand upon his arm, and beckoned him away. He gazed stupidly about him for an instant, and obeyed.

CHARLES DICKENS Oliver Twist

[B]

I would fain linger yet with a few of those among whom I have so long moved, and share their happiness by endeavouring to depict it. I would show Rose Maylie in all the bloom and grace of early womanhood, shedding on her secluded path in life soft and gentle light, that fell on all who trod it with her, and shone into their hearts. I would paint her the life and joy of the fire-side circle and the lively summer group; I would follow her through the sultry fields at noon, and hear the low tones of her sweet voice in the moonlit evening walk; I would watch her in all her goodness and charity abroad, and the smiling untiring discharge of domestic duties at home; I would paint her, and her dead sister's child happy in their love for one another, and passing whole hours together in picturing the friends whom they had so sadly lost; I would summon before me, once again, those joyous little faces that clustered round her knee, and listen to their merry prattle; I would recall the tones of that clear laugh, and conjure up the sympathising tear that glistened in the soft blue eye. These, and a thousand looks and smiles, and turns of thought and speech – I would fain recall them every one.

How Mr Brownlow went on, from day to day, filling the mind of his adopted child with stores of knowledge, and becoming attached to him, more and more, as his nature developed itself, and showed the thriving seeds of all he wished him to become – how he traced in him new traits of his early friend, that awakened in his own bosom old remembrances, melancholy and yet sweet and soothing – how the two orphans, tried by adversity, remembered its lessons in mercy to others, and mutual love, and fervent thanks to Him who had protected and preserved them—these are all matters which need not to be told. I have said that they were truly happy; and without strong affection and humanity of heart, and gratitude to that Being whose code is Mercy, and whose great attribute is Benevolence to all things that breathe, happiness can never be attained.

Within the altar of the old village church there stands a white marble tablet, which bears as yet but one word: 'AGNES'. There is no coffin in that tomb; and may it be many, many years, before another name is placed above it! But, if the spirits of the Dead ever come back to earth, to visit spots hallowed by the love—the love beyond the grave—of those whom they knew in life, I believe that the shade of Agnes sometimes hovers round that solemn nook. I believe it none the less because that nook is in a Church, and she was weak and erring.

CHARLES DICKENS Oliver Twist

[C]

As to conquest, therefore, my Lords, I repeat, it is impossible. You may swell every expense, and every effort, still more extravagantly; pile and accumulate every assistance you can buy or borrow; traffic and barter with every little pitiful German prince, that sells and sends his subjects to the shambles of a foreign prince; your efforts are for ever vain and impotent—doubly so from this mercenary aid on which you rely; for it irritates, to an incurable resentment, the minds of your enemies—to over-run them with the mercenary sons of rapine and plunder; devoting them and their possessions to the rapacity of hireling cruelty! If I were an American, as I am an Englishman, while a foreign troop was landed in my country, I would never lay down my arms—never—never—never.

Your own army is infected with the contagion of these

illiberal allies. The spirit of plunder and of rapine is gone forth among them. I know it–and, notwithstanding what the noble Earl, who moved the Address, has given as his opinion of our American army, I know from authentic information and the most experienced officers, that our discipline is deeply wounded. Whilst this is notoriously our sinking situation, America grows and flourishes: whilst our strength and discipline are lowered, theirs are rising and improving.

But, my Lords, who is the man, that in addition to these disgraces and mischiefs of our army, has dared to authorise and associate to our arms the tomahawk and scalping-knife of the savage? To call into civilised alliance, the wild and inhuman savage of the woods; to delegate to the merciless Indian the defence of disputed rights, and to wage the horrors of his barbarous war against our brethren? My Lords, these enormities cry aloud for redress and punishment; unless thoroughly done away, it will be a stain on the national character–it is a violation of the Constitution–I believe it is against law. It is not the least of our national misfortunes, that the strength and character of our army are thus impaired; infected with the mercenary spirit of robbery and rapine– familiarised to the horrid scenes of savage cruelty, it can no longer boast of the noble and generous principles which dignify a soldier; no longer sympathise with the dignity of the royal banner, nor feel the pride, pomp, and circumstance of glorious war, 'that makes ambition virtue'. What makes ambition virtue?–the sense of honour. But is the sense of honour consistent with the spirit of plunder, or the practice of murder? Can it flow from mercenary motives, or can it prompt to cruel deeds? Besides these murderers and plunder- ers, let me ask our ministers, what other allies have they acquired? What other powers have they associated to their cause? Have they entered into alliance with the king of the gypsies? Nothing, my Lords, is too low or too ludicrous to be consistent with their counsels.

WILLIAM PITT, EARL OF CHATHAM *Speech in the House of Lords*, 20 November 1777

[D]

Of the different passions with which we are born, some are more prevalent at one time, some at another; but experience teaches us that, as they are always antagonistic, they are held in balance by the force of their own opposition. The activity of one motive is corrected by the activity of another. For to every vice there is a corresponding virtue. Cruelty is counteracted by benevolence; sympathy is excited by suffering; the injustice of some provokes the charity of others; new evils are met by new remedies, and even the most enormous offences that have ever been known have left behind them no permanent impression. The desolation of countries and the slaughter of men are losses which never fail to be repaired, and at the distance of a few centuries every vestige of them is effaced. The gigantic crimes of Alexander or Napoleon become after a time void of effect, and the affairs of the world return to their former level. This is the ebb and flow of history, the perpetual flux to which by the laws of our nature we are subject. Above all this, there is a far higher movement; and as the tide rolls on, now advancing, now receeding, there is, amid its endless fluctuations, one thing, and one alone, which endures for ever. The actions of bad men produce only temporary evil, the actions of good men only temporary good; and eventually the good and evil altogether subside, are neutralised by subsequent generations, absorbed by the incessant movement of future ages. But the discoveries of great men never leave us; they are immortal, they contain those eternal truths which survive the shock of empires, outlive the struggles of rival creeds, and witness the decay of successive religions. All these have their different measures and their different standards; one set of opinions for one age, another set for another. They pass away like a dream; they are as the fabric of a vision, which leaves not a rack behind. The discoveries of genius alone remain: it is to them we owe all that we now have, they are for all ages and all times; never young, and never old, they bear the seeds of their own life;

they flow on in a perennial and undying stream; they are essentially cumulative, and, giving birth to the additions which they subsequently receive, they thus influence the most distant posterity, and after the lapse of centuries produce more effect than they were able to do even at the moment of their promulgation.

HENRY THOMAS BUCKLE *History of Civilisation in England*

[E]

Laodamia died; Helen died; Leda, the beloved of Jupiter, went before. It is better to repose in the earth betimes than to sit up late; better, than to cling pertinaciously to what we feel crumbling under us, and to protract an inevitable fall. We may enjoy the present while we are insensible of infirmity and decay: but the present, like a note in music, is nothing but as it appertains to what is past and what is to come. There are no fields of amaranth on this side of the grave: there are no voices, O Rhodope! that are not soon mute, however tuneful: there is no name, with whatever emphasis of passionate love repeated, of which the echo is not faint at last.

W. S. LANDOR *Imaginary Conversations*

[F]

These first tracts of Jura differ in many pleasant ways from the limestone levels round Ingleborough, which are their English types. The Yorkshire moors are mostly by a hundred or two feet higher, and exposed to drift of rain under violent, nearly constant wind. They break into wide fields of loose blocks, and rugged slopes of shale; and are mixed with sands and clay from the millstone grit, which nourish rank grass, and lodge in occasional morass: the wild winds also forbidding any vestige or comfort of tree, except here and there in a sheltered nook of new plantation. But the Jura sky is as calm and clear as that of the rest of France; if the day is bright on the plain, the bounding hills are bright also; the Jura rock, balanced in the make of it between chalk and marble, weathers indeed into curious rifts and furrows, but rarely breaks loose, and has long ago clothed itself either with forest flowers, or with sweet short grass, and all blossoms that love sunshine. The pure air, even on this lower ledge of a thousand feet above sea, cherishes their sweetest scents and liveliest colours, and the winter gives them rest under thawless serenity of snow.

A still greater and stranger difference exists in the system of streams. For all their losing themselves and hiding, and intermitting, their presence is distinctly felt on a Yorkshire moor; one sees the places they have been in yesterday, the wells where they will flow after the next shower, and a trinklet here at the bottom of a crag, or a tinkle there from the top of it, is always making one think whether this is one of the sources of Aire, or rootlets of Ribble, or beginnings of Bolton Strid, or threads of silver which are to be spun into Tees.

But no whisper, nor murmur, nor patter, nor song, of streamlet disturbs the enchanted silence of open Jura. The rain-cloud clasps her cliffs, and floats along her fields; it passes, and in an hour the rocks are dry, and only beads of dew left in the Alchemilla leaves, – but of rivulet, or brook, – no vestige yesterday, or today, or tomorrow. Through unseen fissures and filmy crannies the waters of cliff and plain have alike vanished, only far down in the depths of the main valley glides the strong river, unconscious of change.

JOHN RUSKIN *Praeterita*

9
Final judgment

In Section 5 the stages of the critical sequence were outlined thus:
I RECEPTION OF THE TEXT: first, and as far as possible, un-prejudiced response to the passage as a whole. Initial impact received and stored for critical examination.
II ANALYSIS: (a) sense; (b) tone; (c) intention; (d) what kind of writing is this?; (e) diction; (f) imagery, and (g) rhythms – considered in relation to intention (seen, in other words, as means to ends).
III FINAL JUDGMENT: in which the critic's own opinion of, and response to, the text is expressed; and in the formulation of which the analytical processes of Stage II are constantly referred to.

It has been emphasised that the impressions received during the first reading of the text are scrutinised during Stage II, the critic then searching for those linguistic features that support his first impressions. In this scrutiny, it has been said, he may confirm, reject, or modify the 'label' that he first attached to the text – the subjective elements in the first critical stage (reception) giving direction to the whole analysis; and the analysis itself constantly referring back to – monitoring and being monitored by – the reception. Throughout the analytical stage, the critic is searching the text for the uses of language that support and clarify his responses, being at all times ready to modify or reject those responses for which he is unable to discover adequate textual support.

The critic should consider the writer's choice of language under these headings: diction; imagery; rhythms. The order in which he proceeds will be varied according to his personal preference or the particular features of a given text. No one element can be treated in isolation, for the 'style' of a text is a fusion of all its elements; but a sequential approach enables the critic to be thorough in method and proportioned in judgment.

The last stage, the final judgment, blends the objective and the subjective elements in criticism, referring to and springing out of the closely observed results of the analyses of Stage II, and at the same time presenting the critic's own judgment of the writer's purposes and achievement.

An 'absolute objectivity' is neither possible nor desirable in criticism. However far away from or close to his first impressions his final judgment may be, the critic must, in the end, express *his* opinion: an opinion modified by the objective assessments of the analytical stage, but unavoidably and desirably the product of the intellect, imagination, taste, and experience of the individual reader-critic.

The critic at work

The examples with commentary that follow are intended to help the reader to make his own experiments. They are offered as guides, not as models. The various stages of the critical sequence are indicated. This is for the sake of clarity and as a demonstration of the approach advocated and of the techniques suggested throughout this book. In 'practical criticism' it is the final judgment alone that is 'shown'. The first two stages might be regarded as the critic's 'rough work': the final judgment is the finished product.

The notes that appear under the headings RECEPTION and ANALYSIS are not complete: they are starting points from which each reader may begin his own critical journeys. It would have been tedious to reiterate such questions as: *What other examples can you find? Do you agree with this judgment? Is this comment soundly based on the writer's use of language?* But these questions are implied at every stage, for it is my hope that the reader will be critical of my suggestions and will supplement and correct them.

EXAMPLES WITH COMMENTARY

[A]

But how shall we excuse the supine inattention of the Pagan and philosophic world, to those evidences which were presented by the hand of Omnipotence, not to their reason, but to their senses? During the age of Christ, of his apostles, and of their first disciples, the doctrine which they preached was confirmed by innumerable prodigies. The lame walked, the blind saw, the sick were healed, the dead were raised, demons expelled, and the laws of Nature were frequently suspended for the benefit of the church. But the sages of Greece and Rome turned aside from the awful spectacle, and pursuing the ordinary occupations of life and study, appeared unconscious of any alterations in the moral or physical government of the world. Under the reign of Tiberius, the whole earth, or at least a celebrated province of the Roman empire, was involved in a preternatural darkness of three hours. Even this miraculous event, which ought to have excited the wonder, the curiosity, and the devotion of mankind, passed without notice in an age of science and history. It happened during the lifetime of Seneca and the elder Pliny, who must have experienced the immediate effects, or received the earliest intelligence, of the prodigy. Each of these philosophers, in a laborious work, has recorded all the great phenomena of Nature, earthquakes, meteors, comets, and eclipses, which his indefatigable curiosity could collect. Both the one and the other have omitted to mention the greatest phenomenon to which the mortal eye has been witness since the creation of the globe. A distinct chapter of Pliny is designed for eclipses of an extraordinary nature and unusual duration; but he contents himself with describing the singular defect of light which followed the murder of Caesar, when, during the greatest part of the year, the orb of the sun appeared pale and without splendour. This season of obscurity, which cannot surely be compared with the preternatural darkness of the Passion, had been already celebrated by most of the poets and historians of that memorable age.

EDWARD GIBBON *The Decline and Fall of the Roman Empire*

I RECEPTION

A first impression that Gibbon is mildly wondering at 'the supine inattention of the Pagan and philosophic world', blind to the miraculous evidence of the truth of Christianity, does not last long–does not, in fact, last through the first reading. Certain individual words and phrases appear to signal the obliqueness of the text. The signals are strong enough to indicate the need to hunt for the *real* 'meaning'.

II ANALYSIS

1 Sense. Impossible to separate *what* is said from *how* it is said – for example, how should we read the sentence beginning: 'But the sages of Greece and Rome . . .'? How does Gibbon mean us to interpret this? Throughout the passage he stresses the wisdom and learning of the age (*sages . . . an age of science and learning . . . philosophers . . . indefatigable curiosity . . .*) and *yet* he reports that the most remarkable event of the time went unnoticed.

2 Tone. 'Feeds back' into (1). Perhaps the crucial section is from *The lame walked* to *the moral and physical government of the world*. If 'the laws of Nature were frequently suspended for the benefit of the church' *could* sages turn aside? How *could* wise men – men of science – men capable of laborious work – men filled with indefatigable curiosity – be unconscious of 'alterations in the moral and physical government of the world'? So far from expressing wonder at the inattention of the contemporary world, is not Gibbon nudging his readers into questioning whether there was anything in the Christian case to excite the attention of the philosophers? The tone, in fact, is ironic – the whole passage is oblique: he states one thing, but means another.

3 Intention. He intends, therefore, by indirect methods to push his reader into a coolly sceptical position. He challenges the miraculous evidence for Christianity, but avoids a direct confrontation with orthodoxy.

4 What kind of writing is this? (a) It is clearly not fiction! The title tells us that it is the work of an historian, though the contents of the passage seem to be argumentative, persuasive or controversial rather than narrative. (b) The title, again, supplies the period – second half of the eighteenth century – but what linguistic features support this? Diction? Sentence structure? Tone, perhaps? – does the passage represent a particular way of looking at its subject that is characteristic of its period? (c) The treatment of the subject has been partly suggested under (a) and (b): it is polemical. (d) The language is essentially written, not spoken, and (e) it exhibits a marked degree of formality – no colloquialisms – a polished and considered piece of writing.

5 Diction. It seems best to start the 'method' analysis with this, since it was particular words and phrases (rather than imagery or rhythm) that stood out during the first reading. Bearing in mind

what has been said about Gibbon's intention, consider the following, both in their immediate context and in relation to the passage
as a whole:

> supine . . . the hand of Omnipotence . . . innumerable prod-
> igies . . . awful spectacle . . . preternatural (twice used) . . .
> excited . . . the prodigy . . . the greatest phenomenon to which
> mortal eye has been witness since the creation of the globe . . .
> singular defect of light . . . season of obscurity . . .

Detailed examination is, of course, necessary, but it may be
helpful to suggest that there is a twofold effect here: (*a*) precision
in the use of individual words; (*b*) a cumulative emotional impact
derived from the sequence of exactly used Latinised polysyllables.
Gibbon is at once meticulous and suggestive. Precise reference and
emotive force are combined. Note especially, as an example, the
contrast between 'singular defect of light' and 'preternatural
darkness of the Passion'.

6 *Imagery*. Vestigial. Effect of darkness built up, however. How?
To what end? Possibly one of the most powerful elements in the
obliqueness of the passage – is Gibbon, by implication, transferring
the 'darkness' from the Pagan world to the Christian? (This would,
of course, involve both the literal and the metaphorical use of the
word 'darkness'). What does the darkness symbolise?

7 *Rhythms*. (*a*) Syntactical elements: some examples of balanced
repetitions, e.g. *not to . . ./but to; who must have experienced . . ./or
(who must have) received. . . .* Graphic plots show a fondness for this
effect:

(*b*) Stress elements: the most remarkable rhythmic device is
achieved by clusters of stresses. A dominantly two-stressed rhythm
(the stresses are distributed, not syllabic):

> Both the one | and the other | have omitted to mention | the
> greatest phenomenon | to which the mortal eye | has been
> witness | since the creation of the globe |

is occasionally and surprisingly over-ridden by a remarkable alternation of compression and diffusion. For example, the sentence beginning: *The lame walked* ... has closely clustered two-stress groups up to *and*, after which word the coupled stresses are more widely separated:

$$// \backslash // / \backslash // \backslash // \backslash // \backslash // | \text{ and } | // | // | // |$$

Compare the sentence beginning: *Each of these philosophers* ... where the stress-clustering occurs in the middle:

←Diffused stresses →	←Compressed stresses →	←Diffused stresses ——→
Each ... Nature	earthquakes ... eclipses	which ... collect

It is chiefly by the use of this device that Gibbon slows or quickens the pace of his prose while keeping within the tight framework of the two-stress rhythm. His purposes in this passage obviously require a disciplined pattern, but he moves easily within it.

(*c*) Pitch elements: pitch curves are an interesting feature of the rhythms. Take, again, as an example, the sentence beginning: *The lame walked* ... and notice how pitch and stress interact (five upward curves with clustered stresses; three downward curves with diffused stresses):

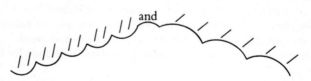

Rhythmic effects such as this—and there are many other examples in the passage—are a powerful reinforcement of the diction and vestigial imagery; all three communicating, in combination, the strong emotion that underlies the apparently cool and essentially rational approach of the 'surface meaning'.

III FINAL JUDGMENT

This text is a most skilful example of polemical writing, achieving its effect by means of a delicate yet deadly irony. At first sight, it appears that Gibbon is rebuking the Greek and Roman philosophers and historians for their blindness to the miraculous evidences of Christian truth. This immediate impression is soon modified, however, 'Supine inattention' contrasts with 'sages' and 'study'; a 'miraculous event' passes unnoticed 'in an age of science and history'; industrious scholars characterised by 'indefatigable curiosity' record 'a singular defect of light which followed the murder of Caesar' yet ignore the 'preternatural darkness of the Passion'.

Thus, insistence upon the wisdom and learning of the age stands in marked contrast to its astonishing blindness in one respect. A period distinguished for its learning was apparently unconscious of fundamental changes that had occured in 'the moral or physical government of the world'. That paradox is the key to Gibbon's real meaning and purpose.

Once the paradox is grasped, the tone comes through clearly. The writer's emotions are strong, but controlled; his irony is serious, not playful; his intention is to expose folly, though he feints before delivering his thrusts.

The Latinised language is employed with fastidious precision, and the complexity of the task undertaken by Gibbon absolves him from any charge of pedantry in his employment of a learned and wide-ranging diction. A difficult intellectual feat may well justify the use of recondite expression. Lucidity and energy characterise both the choice of words and their arrangement, and the sensitive handling of language is well demonstrated by the subtle contrasts established between, say, 'singular defect of light' and 'preternatural darkness of the Passion'; by the careful distinctions of meaning in 'the wonder, the curiosity, and the devotion of mankind'; by the descriptive skill of 'the orb of the sun appeared pale and without splendour'.

The imagery is vestigial, for the language is literal rather than metaphoric. Yet a strong impression of darkness is created: a darkness that assumes a symbolic force which Gibbon cunningly aims, not at his apparent target, the pagan philosophers, but at his real mark, those who believe in the miracles of the early Christian era.

The sonorous quality of the polysyllables fits the weightiness of the theme, and the remarkable handling of rhythms reveals an ease of movement that signals agility of intellect. The combination of pitch curves and stress clusters (see, for example, the sentence

99

beginning: *The lame walked . . .*) though, doubtless, the result of infinite care in composition gives an impression both of masterly control and fluency of expression. This command of subtle and varied rhythms (contrast with the example just chosen the sentence beginning: *Each of these philosophers . . .*) reinforces the sense of intellectual authority that it must be part of his purpose to create.

Perhaps the most remarkable feature of this text is the emotional impact that writing, apparently so rational, so cool, can make. The sureness of Gibbon's control of his linguistic resources – and the extent and variety of those resources – enables him to voice his attack upon superstition without excitement, yet with conviction. His voice is never raised, yet he enunciates forcefully his contempt for an ignorance that masquerades as faith. This is the writing of a man who cares passionately for truth, yet is controlled and rational in the expression of his deep concern.

But even Gibbon must depend upon the vigilance of his readers, and the sophistication of his methods may be self-defeating. He demands much: close attention, mental agility, and intellectual energy. Irony is a two-edged sword that sometimes cuts its wielder; and Gibbon's virtuosity has its dangers. In his own day he was thanked by a Bishop for his defence of miracles; and it could perhaps be argued that he might have achieved more had he spoken out.

Yet – even though his most devoted admirers may question whether he was not, at times, almost over-exquisite – to those with a taste for it, this is incomparable writing.

[B]

There are two things to do. Strip off at once all the ideal drapery from nationality, from nations, peoples, states, empires, and even from Internationalism and Leagues of Nations. Leagues of Nations should be just flatly and simply committees where representatives of the various business houses, so-called Nations, meet and consult. Consultations, board-meetings of the State business men: no more. *Representatives of Peoples* – who can represent me? – I am myself. I don't intend anybody to represent me.

You, you Cabinet Minister–what are you? You are the arch-grocer, the super-hotel-manager, the foreman over the ships and railways. What else are you? You are the super-tradesman, same paunch, same ingratiating manner, same everything. Governments, what are they? Just board-meetings of big business men. Very useful, too–very thankful we are that somebody *will* look after this business. But Ideal! An Ideal Government? What nonsense. We might as well talk of an Ideal Cook's Tourist Agency, or an Ideal Achille Serre Cleaners and Dyers. Even the ideal Ford of America is only an ideal *average* motor-car. His employees are not spontaneous, nonchalant human beings, à la Whitman. They are just well-tested, well-oiled sections of the Ford automobile.

Politics–what are they? Just another, extra-large, commercial wrangle over buying and selling–nothing else. Very good to have the wrangle. Let us have the buying and selling well done. But *ideal!* Politics *ideal! Political idealists!* What rank gewgaw and nonsense! We have just enough sense not to talk Ideal Selfridges or Ideal Krupps or Ideal Heidsiecks. Then let us have enough sense to drop the ideal of England or Europe or anywhere else. Let us be men and women, and keep our house in order. But let us pose no longer as houses, or as England, or as housemaids, or as democrats.

Pull the ideal drapery off Governments, States, Nations, and Inter-nations. Show them for what they are: big business concerns for manufacturing and retailing Standard goods. Put up a statue of the Average Man, something like those abominable statues of men in woollen underwear which surmount a shop at the corner of Oxford Street and Totten-ham Court Road. Let your statue be grotesque: in fact, borrow those ignominious statues of men in pants and vests: the fat one for Germany, the thin one for England, the middling one for France, the gaunt one for America. Point to these statues, which guard the entrance to the House of Commons, to the Chamber, to the Senate, to the Reichstag–

and let every Prime Minister and President know the quick of his own ignominy. Let every bursting politician see himself in his commercial pants. Let every senatorial idealist and saviour of mankind be reminded that his office depends on the quality of the underwear he supplies to the State. Let every fiery and rhetorical Deputy remember that he is only held together by his patent suspenders.

And then, when the people of the world have finally got over the state of giddy idealising of governments, nations, inter-nations, politics, democracies, empires, and so forth; when they really understand that their collective activities are only cook-housemaid to their sheer individual activities; when they at last calmly accept a business concern for what it is; then, at last, we may actually see free men in the streets.

D. H. LAWRENCE *Democracy*
[from *Phoenix*]

I RECEPTION
The excited quality of the writing is the first thing that strikes the reader: a breathless, intensely personal utterance, so subjective that one is disinclined to believe that anything said about politics in this manner can have a serious application; or can, indeed, be meant as anything more than a rather irritable, though often amusing outburst. Depending on how seriously the individual reader takes politics – what his attitudes to it are, or what he thinks they ought to be – he may experience either irritation or amusement as he first reads this passage.

II ANALYSIS
1 *Sense*. The impression that a reader seriously interested in politics cannot take this passage seriously is soon revealed as the merely prejudiced response that it is. Close reading of the text shows that Lawrence cares intensely about his theme, and that the whole sense of the passage is summed up in the climactic paragraph: 'And then, when the people of the world ... we may actually see free men in the streets.' He is, in fact, arguing the necessity of a new and responsible attitude to politics.
2 *Tone*. There is anger here: 'But *ideal*! Politics *ideal*! *Political*

idealists!'; and mockery: 'Let every bursting politician see himself in his commercial pants.' And the anger stems from—and the mockery is used to advance—Lawrence's conviction that there must be a better way. What comes through in the end is a desperate sincerity.

3 *Intention*. Very largely revealed under (1) and (2) above. Lawrence wants to shock, mock, and persuade us out of what he regards as a false and, therefore, dangerous attitude. He must, he believes, strip away illusion and force us to face the truth about ourselves.

4 *What kind of writing is this?* (*a*) The genre is, in a way, difficult to define, because the word 'essay' is associated with academic lucubrations that seem to belong to another world than this excited outburst. Yet no other description is free from even more serious objections, so 'essay' it must be. (*b*) The dates of Lawrence's birth and death (1885–1930) supply the chronological limits for the period of composition, but internal evidence—particularly vocabulary and sentence construction—makes it clear that this is 'modern', i.e. written after the first world war. (So, of course, do some of the historical references.) Even more telling is the way in which Lawrence approaches this subject, with an irreverent, iconoclastic impatience. (*c*) The topic of discourse is politics; a fact which may lead to unjustified assumptions on the reader's part, and he may—according to his own attitude to the subject (see end of 1 above)—be sidetracked in his criticism unless he is objective in his analyses. (*d*) The language must belong to the written mode rather than the spoken (see genre) but it is obvious that Lawrence wrote much of this as if he were speaking it. He wants us to hear his voice as we read. See, especially, the last sentence of paragraph 1, where an interrogatory and exclamatory note is sounded. (There are many other examples.) (*e*) Consequently, the language is informal and so free from constraint that it gives an impression of colloquialism, suitable to a rapidly-moving monologue: an impression strengthened by the many verbless sentences.

5 *Diction*. The choice of words is chiefly remarkable for its variety, seeming to be drawn from a vocabulary essentially that of a working writer. There is no compartmentalisation here: no sense that the nature of the subject imposes conventional restraints. The word that is used is the word that is needed, regardless of its origin.

So, *ideal* is used in a particular way, in its 'philosophical' sense; but *pants*, *vests* and *suspenders* are felt to be equally at home in a passage expounding serious ideas about a serious subject. Other examples readily illustrate this range and variety – this uninhibited use of language: 'ingratiating . . . nonchalant . . . abominable . . . grotesque . . . ignominious . . . paunch . . . nonsense . . . wrangle . . . rank . . . giddy . . .' The impression given is that of a quick-thinking man, whose energetic mind is impatient of 'literary' restrictions and whose ready pen will not be checked by considerations of what is 'proper' to his subject. (Query: would not *tongue* perhaps be a better word than *pen*?) The word he wants is the word that he will use, and he does not have to search for it. Indeed, he will often compound a vocabulary for his own use: 'arch-grocer . . . super-hotel-manager . . . super-tradesman . . . cook-house-maid . . . bursting politician . . . commercial pants . . .' An unusually vivid effect is produced: 'We have just enough sense not to talk of Ideal Selfridges . . . abominable statues of men in woollen underwear . . . know the quick of his own ignominy . . .'

6 *Imagery*. Though there are no outstanding examples of indivi-dual images, the whole passage turns on a metaphor. This is clearly seen if one divides the text into two halves. The text, in fact, is structured by Lawrence quite deliberately in two sections:

(a) From the beginning to the end of the third paragraph.
(b) The last two paragraphs.

Both halves begin with the same fiery command: 'Strip off at once all the ideal drapery . . ./Pull the ideal drapery off . . .' The first section bludgeons the reader into a recognition that the *idealised* conceptions of nationality, nations, peoples, states, empires, Cabinet Ministers, governments, etc, are lies: draperies covering the naked truth. The second section, having reiterated the opening metaphor, continues with a reference to the statue of the Average Man 'something like those abominable statues of men in woollen underwear . . .' Then, in a series of rapid exhortations, Lawrence verbally strips the important men of the world – our governors – down to their pants. This metaphorical continuation of the argument of the first section culminates in the passionate statement of the last clause. The whole passage, in fact, is a denunciation of sham; a fervent contrasting of what things *seem* with what they *are*; an eloquent sermon on the text: *See – if you would be free*.

7 Rhythms. Little use is made of syntactical repetitions. The careful parallels and formal balances of the earlier ages of English prose are absent. This is to be expected: Lawrence's excited spontaneity could not be communicated in such a framework. Nevertheless, the last paragraph affords a striking example of a careful syntactical structure:

(*a*) And *then*, when the people of the world . . .

   (*b*) when they really understand . . .

      (*c*) when they at last . . .

         (*d*) then, at last, we may actually see free men . . .

The whole of that paragraph is, in fact, a sustained periodic sentence, the main statement being held off until the last clause. Following that clue, we see that the whole of the second section of the text is constructed in exactly the same way, for every sentence is preparatory to–annunciatory of–that climactic last clause.

The structure of the passage as a whole affords a striking illustration of 'audible shape': (i) First section–a series of loose, staccato sentences. (ii) Second section–in effect, one long periodic sentence. A graphic plot of the whole structure reveals this shape:

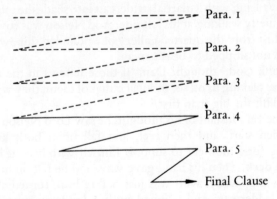

An overall structure admirably fitted to, and shaped by, Lawrence's rhetoric.

Stress and pitch elements within this structure are dominant over syntax. Verbless sentences, as we have noticed, are frequent; and the thudding and clustered stresses of the first section play an important part in Lawrence's shock tactics (sentence 2 is a good example). In the second section there is more variety. Stresses are compressed at first: diffused in the long fourth sentence of paragraph four: cluster again: then thin out again, before the final paragraph reveals so remarkably Lawrence's rhythmic suppleness. The rise and fall of stress-supported pitch curves in that paragraph merits close attention and accurate plotting.

III FINAL JUDGMENT

Use the above notes, supplementing and modifying them in accordance with your own response to the text, as the basis for a final judgment of the Lawrence passage.

[C]

Lord Nelson had just made a little joke, such as he often indulged in, not from any carelessness about the scene around him–which was truly awful–but simply to keep up his spirits, and those of his brave and beloved companion. Captain Hardy, a tall and portly man, clad in bright uniform, and advancing with a martial stride, cast into shade the mighty hero quietly walking at his left side. And Nelson was covered with dust from the quarter-gallery of a pounded ship, which he had not stopped to brush away.

'Thank God,' thought Dan, 'if those fellows in the tops, who are picking us off so, shoot at either of them, they will be sure to hit the big man first.'

In the very instant of his thought, he saw Lord Nelson give a sudden start, and then reel, and fall upon both knees, striving for a moment to support himself with his one hand on the deck. Then his hand gave way, and he fell on his left side, while Hardy, who was just before him, turned at the cabin ladderway, and stopped with a loud cry over him. Dan ran up, and placed his bare arms under the wounded shoulder, and helped to raise and set him on his staggering legs.

'I hope you are not much hurt, my lord?' said the Captain, doing his best to smile.

'They have done for me at last,' the hero gasped. 'Hardy, my backbone is shot through.'

Through the roar of battle, sobs of dear love sounded along the blood-stained deck, as Dan and another seaman took the pride of our nation tenderly, and carried him down to the orlop-deck. Yet even so, in the deadly pang and draining of the life-blood, the sense of duty never failed, and the love of country conquered death. With his feeble hand he contrived to reach the handkerchief in his pocket, and spread it over his face and breast, lest the crew should be disheartened.

'I know who fired that shot,' cried Dan, when he saw that he could help no more. 'He shall never live to boast of it, if I have to board the French ship to fetch him.'

He ran back quickly to the quarter-deck, and there found three or four others eager to give their lives for Nelson's death. The mizzen-top of the *Redoubtable*, whence the fatal shot had come, was scarcely so much as fifty feet from the starboard rail of the *Victory*. The men who were stationed in that top, although they had no brass cohorn there, such as those in the main and fore tops plied, had taken many English lives, while the thick smoke surged around them.

For some time they had worked unheeded in the louder roar of cannon, and when at last they were observed, it was hard to get a fair shot at them, not only from the rolling of the entangled ships, and clouds of blinding vapour, but because they retired out of sight to load, and only came forward to catch their aim. However, by the exertions of our marines—who should have been at them long ago—these sharpshooters from the coign of vantage were now reduced to three brave fellows. They had only done their duty, and perhaps had no idea how completely they had done it; but naturally enough our men looked at them as if they were 'too bad for hanging'. Smoky as the air was, the three men saw that a very strong feeling was aroused against them, and that none of their own side was at hand to back them up. And the language of the English—though they could not understand it—was clearly that of bitter condemnation.

The least resolute of them became depressed by this, being doubtless a Radical who had been taught that *Vox populi* is *Vox Dei*. He endeavoured, therefore, to slide down the rigging, but was shot through the heart, and dead before he had time to know it. At the very same moment the most desperate villain of the three – as we should call him – or the most heroic of these patriots (as the French historians describe him) popped forward and shot a worthy Englishman, who was shaking his fist instead of pointing his gun.

Then an old Quartermaster, who was standing on the poop, with his legs spread out as comfortably as if he had his Sunday dinner on the spit before him, shouted – 'That's him, boys – that glazed hat beggar! Have at him all together, next time he comes forrard.' As he spoke, he fell dead, with his teeth in his throat, from the fire of the other Frenchman. But the carbine dropped from the man who had fired, and his body fell dead as the one he had destroyed, for a sharp little Middy, behind the Quartermaster, sent a bullet through the head, as the hand drew trigger. The slayer of Nelson remained alone, and he kept back warily where none could see him.

'All of you fire, quick one after the other,' cried Dan, who had picked up a loaded musket, and was kneeling in the embrasure of a gun; 'fire so that he may tell the shots; that will fetch him out again. Sing out first, 'There he is! as if you saw him.'

The men on the quarter-deck and poop did so, and the Frenchman, who was watching through a hole, came forward for a safe shot while they were loading. He pointed the long gun which had killed Nelson at the smart young officer on the poop, but the muzzle flew up ere he pulled the trigger, and leaning forward he fell dead, with his arms and legs spread, like a jack for oiling axles. Dan had gone through some small-arm drill in the fortnight he spent at Portsmouth, and his eyes were too keen for the bull's-eye. With a rest for his muzzle he laid it truly for the spot where the Frenchman would reappear; with extreme punctuality he shot him in the throat; and the gallant man who deprived the world of Nelson was thus despatched to a better one, three hours in front of his victim.

R. D. BLACKMORE *Springhaven*

I RECEPTION

First impressions are mixed and contrasting. The strong narrative flow arouses interest and gives pleasure; but there are frequent checks. The passage seems to halt from time to time, as if the writer had lost sight of his real purposes and was unsure of his intended effects. These points must obviously be investigated closely during analysis and an attempt must be made to account for the reader's uneasiness. Is the text less direct than it appears to be?

II ANALYSIS

1 *Sense*. The story told is easily summarised: 'the death of Nelson and the subsequent killing of the Frenchman who shot him.'

2 *Tone*. This is far from easy to determine, and it is here that the critic must begin to grapple with the ambiguities of response noted under 1 above. As the teller of a stirring story dealing with the death of a national hero, Blackmore's seriousness of intention should be indisputable. The first part of the passage (to the end of the third paragraph) is in what we take to be the right key. Difficulties of interpretation arise after this point. What are we to make of 'doing his best to smile'? The effect is comic, but that could hardly have been the intention? What *was* the intention? The serious note is broken again in the paragraph beginning: 'For some time . . .', the 'too bad for hanging' remark being very hard to take. Harder still, is the assessment of the effect that Blackmore hoped for in writing those words. He weights them with the quotation marks, so he clearly intended some special effect. Again, at the beginning of the next paragraph ('being doubtless a Radical who had been taught . . .') the tone and the intention are uncertain. Perhaps a grim humour? That same paragraph ends with a sentence that defies interpretation: balance–reasonableness–sense of proportion–followed by humour? The next paragraph ('Then an old Quartermaster . . .') introduces a deliberately comic effect ('legs spread out as comfortably as if . . .'), immediately

followed by an attempt at grim realism ('his teeth in his throat . . .'). The 'in slang' of 'sharp little Middy' is presumably intended to strengthen the realism – to convey the impression that the writer knows all about the Navy? The narrative is strong again from this point, but there is dilution of interest again in the last paragraph, and the tone is once more uncertain at the end: ' with *extreme punctuality* he shot him in the throat . . .'/'the gallant man . . .'

3 Intention. The narrative content makes the 'functional intention' plain: to tell an exciting story; but the tonal uncertainties (see *2* above) introduce problems of interpretation. How can we be sure of Blackmore's *full* intention? How do we know what he wanted his readers to *feel* about the story he was telling? Desirable though it is for the critic to have established intention fully by this stage of the criticism – so that the 'means-to-ends' analyses of diction, imagery and rhythms are fruitful – there seems little chance of certainty as yet in this case. Full understanding of intention will perhaps be reached through the close text work of the analytical stage.

4 What kind of writing is this? (*a*) The text is taken from an historical novel, the juxtaposing of fictitious and historical characters being a common feature of this kind of fiction from Scott onwards. (*b*) The period is, as Blackmore's dates (1825–1900) prove, mid- to late-nineteenth century, and the general linguistic features bear this out. The passage has an essentially pre-1914 flavour in diction and sentence construction and contains some old-fashioned turns of phrase – 'catch their aim'; 'tell the shots'. (*c*) Standard English is chiefly used, with variations for special purposes: eg technical terms such as 'cohorn' and 'orlop-deck' to establish authenticity; 'that glazed hat beggar' and 'forrard' to establish the social rank and occupation of the old Quartermaster. (*d*) The passage is narrative, with brief interludes for character-drawing and reflection. (*e*) The language is part-written, part-spoken; and (*f*) it varies from the informality of spoken language in *parts* of the dialogue to a high degree of formality in some of the descriptive and reflective passages: 'Yet even so . . . lest the crew should be disheartened'; '. . . being doubtless a Radical . . . *Vox Dei*.'

The analysis of the kind of writing has done something to help to solve the problems left open under *3* (*Intention*). It is now clear that Blackmore may legitimately have aimed at achieving several different effects, for the genre invites variety.

The critical problem presented by this text may well become focussed on the writer's ability to impose a unity of impression on these diverse elements. This, in turn, may prove to depend upon the relationship between the referential and the emotive uses of the language employed in the text.

5 *Diction*. The elusive and ambiguous tonal qualities were connected with particular words and phrases. Method analysis should, therefore, begin with diction. A rigorous attempt must be made to clarify the initial responses and to resolve the perplexities of interpretation. Following up the preliminary analyses, we note a frequent use of technical terms: 'quarter-gallery', 'Orlop-deck'; 'mizzen-top', 'cohorn' (*grenade projector*), etc. This is, of course, legitimate in view of Blackmore's subject-matter and purposes, but we have already been made uncomfortable by 'sharp little Middy' and now notice a probable confusion between 'small-arm drill' and 'musketry'–the latter being, in all probability, the term that Blackmore really wanted. Again, does a writer who knows this subject refer to '*pulling* the trigger' or use such an expression as 'the *hand drew* trigger'? Doubts of this kind may be trifling or important; but doubt, once admitted, must be explored and either confirmed or refuted. The area of doubt spreads over from the use of technical terms to the emotive language. Further consideration of 'doing his best to smile' and 'sobs of dear love' seems necessary. So, too, Dan's 'cry' as he is running back to the quarter-deck must be evaluated. Is it true? And what about 'three or four others eager to give their *lives* for Nelson's *death*'? Again, see the end of the tenth paragraph: 'popped forward . . . worthy Englishman . . . shaking his fist instead of pointing his gun'.

The lines along which enquiry may proceed have been indicated, and so we may turn to:

6 *Imagery*. Chiefly vestigial and descriptive, but there are two images to which Blackmore obviously attached importance. We have already quoted and questioned the appropriateness of 'his legs spread out as comfortably as if he had his Sunday dinner on the spit before him'. (See Section 7 again. Consider the tenor, vehicle and ground of the image.) The other occurs in the last paragraph: '. . . he fell dead, with his arms and legs spread, like a jack for oiling axles.' The general sense is clear, but the force has leaked out with the passage of time. The reader may have seen such an

object in a museum. If so, he can, with an effort, recreate the image; if not, the image is dead. (Dead, too, is the laboured Shakespearian allusion: 'coign of vantage'.) Deadness is the characteristic quality of the imagery. Where in the passage does Blackmore succeed in making us see, hear, smell, touch or taste vividly? Even where he makes his most strenuous efforts, his imagery is weak because its referential basis is imprecise.

7 *Rhythms*. Unremarkable. The chief constructional characteristic is the frequent use of adjectival modifiers: 'Captain Hardy, a tall and portly man, clad in bright uniform, and advancing with a martial stride, cast into shade the mighty hero quietly walking at his left side.' The result is an ugly 'stopping and starting'. Rhythmic flow hardly exists and – where rapid action is described – Blackmore's fondness for asides of all kinds often clutters the prose line.

III FINAL JUDGMENT

The unease experienced at the first reading of this narrative persists. Blackmore's failure arises from inadequacy of experience and uncertainty of intention. The subject matter demands accurate knowledge if the writer is to involve the reader in the events and emotions depicted. (It would be an informative critical exercise to compare C. S. Forester's aims and methods with those of Blackmore.) The mere act of sprinkling the description with technical terms is not sufficient to achieve credibility, especially when the terms are not always accurately applied.

The pseudo-emotive hotchpotch arises from this failure to treat a realised experience truthfully. Blackmore is too patently guessing about events that he has never experienced and about people whom he cannot create. Careful study of each description of violent death in the passage shows him up all too clearly as a fraud: he knows nothing of battle and his approach to war is that of an armchair warrior or a senile fire-eater.

The writing is flaccid, for the diction is cliché-ridden, the imagery opaque, and rhythms nerveless. This linguistic failure accurately mirrors the feebleness of the impulse that moved the writer. He had nothing to say about the subject he chose, and the vacuity of his mind is inevitably reflected in the forced jokes and false emotions.

On the evidence of this passage it would be fair to credit him with some skill in story-telling; but his uncertainty of purpose, his emotional immaturity and his lack of taste are fatal to the larger ambitions he appears to have entertained.

FOR PRACTICE

The following selection of passages will provide further experience of the criticism of prose. The passages vary considerably in length and afford critical material suitable either for rapid practice or for sustained study. Some of the authors are named, some are anonymous; and from Passage 4 onwards the texts are printed in chronological order. If desired, the longer passages may be taken paragraph by paragraph to provide shorter critical exercises. Practice in summarising complex arguments is also afforded.

1

From this time, it seems, I was disposed of to a beggar woman that wanted a pretty little child to set out her case; and after that, to a gipsy, under whose government I continued until I was about six years old; and this woman, though I was continually dragged about with her from one part of the country to another, yet never let me want for anything; and I called her mother, though she told me at last that she was not my mother, but that she bought me for twelve shillings of another woman, who told her how she came by me, and told her that my name was Bob Singleton, not Robert, but plain Bob; for it seems they never knew by what name I was christened.

It is in vain to reflect here what a terrible fright the careless hussy was in that lost me; what treatment she received from my justly-enraged father and mother, and the horror these must be in at the thoughts of their child being thus carried away; for, as I never knew anything of the matter, but just what I have related, nor who my father and mother were, so it would make but a needless digression to talk of it here.

My good gipsy mother, for some of her worthy actions no doubt, happened in the process of time to be hanged; and, as this fell out something too soon for me to be perfected in the strolling trade, the parish where I was left, which, for my life, I cannot remember, took some care of me to be sure; for the first thing I can remember of myself afterwards was, that I went to a parish school, and the minister of the parish used to talk to me to be a good boy; and that, though I was but a poor boy, if I minded my book, and served God, I might make a good man.

2

Later he was to be famous and honoured throughout the South Caribbean; he was to be a hero of the people and, after that, a British representative at Lake Success. But when I first met him he was still a struggling masseur, at a time when masseurs were ten a penny in Trinidad.

This was just at the beginning of the war, when I was still at school. I had been bullied into playing football, and in my first game I had been kicked hard on the shin and laid up for weeks afterwards.

My mother distrusted doctors and never took me to one. I am not blaming her for this because in those days people went by preference to the unqualified masseur or the quack dentist.

'I know the sort of doctors it have in Trinidad,' my mother used to say. 'They think nothing of killing two three people before breakfast.'

This wasn't as bad as it sounds: in Trinidad the midday meal is called breakfast.

My foot was hot and swollen, and getting more and more painful. 'So what are we going to do?' I asked.

'Do?' my mother said. 'Do? Give the foot a little more time. You never know what could happen.'

I said, 'I know what going to happen. I going lose the whole damn foot, and you know how these Trinidad doctors like cutting off black people foot.'

My mother grew a little worried and she made a large mud-plaster for the foot that evening.

Two days later she said, 'It looking a little serious. Is only Ganesh now for you, boy.'

'Who the hell is this Ganesh?'

This was a question many people were going to ask later on.

'Who is *this* Ganesh?' my mother mocked. '*This* Ganesh? You see the sort of education they giving you children these days. Your foot break up and hurting, and still you talking about this man as though you is his father when the man old enough to be your father.'

I said, 'What he does do?'

'Oh, he does cure people.'

She spoke in a guarded way and I felt that she didn't want to talk too much about Ganesh because his gift of healing was a holy thing.

It was a long drive to Ganesh's, more than two hours. He lived in a place called Fuente Grove, not far from Princes Town. Fuente Grove—Fountain Grove—seemed a curious name. There was no hint of a fountain anywhere, no hint even of water. For miles around the land was flat, treeless, and hot. You drove through miles and miles of sugar-cane; then the sugar-cane stopped abruptly to make room for Fuente Grove. It was a sad little village, just a dozen or so thatched huts strung out on the edge of the narrow lumpy road. Beharry's shop was the one sign of a social life and we stopped outside it. It was a wooden building, dingy distemper flaking off the walls and the corrugated-iron roof warped and rusted. A little notice said that Beharry was licensed to sell spirituous liquors, and I could see the man so privileged—as I thought—sitting on a stool in front of the counter. Spectacles rested on the tip of his nose and he was reading the *Trinidad Sentinel* at arm's length.

Our taxi-driver shouted, 'Ai!'

The paper was lowered. 'Oi! I is Beharry.' He slid off the stool and began rubbing the palms of his hands over his little belly. 'Is the pundit you looking for, not so?'

The taxi-driver said, 'Nah. We came all the way from Port of Spain just for the scenery.'

Beharry was not prepared for this incivility. He stopped rubbing his belly and started to tuck his vest into his khaki trousers. A big woman appeared from behind the counter and when she saw us she pulled her veil over her head.

'These people want to find out something,' Beharry told her, and went behind the counter.

The woman shouted, 'Who you looking for?'

My mother replied, 'The pundit we looking for.'

'Just go down the road a little bit,' the woman said. 'You can't miss the house. It have a mango tree in the yard.'

The woman was right. We couldn't miss Ganesh's house. It had the only tree in the village and it looked a little better than most of the huts.

The driver honked the horn and a woman appeared from behind the house. She was a young woman, big-boned but thin, and she was trying to give us some attention and shoo away some fowls with a *cocoye* broom at the same time. She examined us for a while and then began shouting, 'Man! Eh, manwa!'

Then she looked hard at us again and pulled her veil over her head.

She shouted again, 'Eh, eh, you aint hear me calling you? Man! Eh, manwa!'

A high voice came fluting out of the house. 'Yes, man.'

The driver turned off the engine and we heard sounds of shuffling inside the house.

Presently a young man came out on the small verandah. He was dressed in the ordinary way, trousers and vest, and I didn't think he looked particularly holy. He wasn't wearing the dhoti and turban I had expected. I was a little reassured when I saw that he was holding a big book. To look at us he had to shelter his eyes from the glare with his free hand, and as soon as he saw us he ran down the wooden steps and across the yard and said to my mother, 'Is nice to see you. How is everything these days?'

The taxi-driver, now curiously correct, was staring at the

heat waves jigging up from the black road, and chewing on a match-stick.

Ganesh saw me and said, 'Ooh, ooh, something happen to the boy.' And he made a few sad noises.

v. s. naipaul *The Mystic Masseur*

3

A brilliant November morning with a sky of diamond blue above the bay and the red flowers of a long summer still glowing darkly on the Rock. The intense blackness of the lampless night had rolled away to reveal, incandescent on the northern horizon, the country we had come to seek. It crouched before us in a great ring of lion-coloured mountains, raw, sleeping and savage. There were scarred and crumpled valleys, the sharp peaks wreathed in their dusty fires, and below them the white towns piled high on their little hills and the empty roads running crimson along the faces of the cliffs. Already, across the water, one heard, or fancied one heard, the sobbing of asses, the cries and salty voices cutting through the thin gold air. And from the steep hillside rose a column of smoke, cool as marble, pungent as pine, which hung like a signal over the landscape, obscure, imperative and motionless.

So we left Gibraltar to its trim English streets, to its Genoese money-changers, Maltese tobacconists, Hindu silk-merchants and crook-boned Cockney soldiers, and we went down to the quay and gathered our bags and boarded the ferry for Spain.

The ferry flew the Spanish flag, had paddlewheels, and was old, black-funnelled and squat as a duck. It was the type one might have seen, a hundred years ago, running mission-aries up the Congo, loaded with whips and bibles. But today, being Saturday, it was packed to the rails with smugglers. As we moved across the oil-blue waters, innocent in the naked sun, they disposed their Gibraltar loot about them. Strapped to their limbs, under their clothes, went cigarettes, soap, sweets, tinned milk, coffee, corned beef and jars of jam. Then the port of Algericas drew near, and fishermen cried to us from their boats, and we bounced off a yacht, bumped heavily against the quay, and tied up in a tangle, and landed.

The acid-yellow stones, the quay littered with straw and palms, the green-cloaked policemen carrying pistols, the lax and amiable formalities of passports and customs; then we stood free at last upon the ground, surrounded by Spain and the smell of fish-boxes. I turned then and spoke, after many years, my first words of Spanish, to a porter, and we understood each other. We bargained, our baggage was loaded on to a handcart, and we entered the town.

And here was the scene so long remembered: the bright façades still crumbling in the sun; the beggars crowding the quaysides, picking up heads of fish; the vivid shapely girls, with hair shining like pitch; the tiny delicate-stepping donkeys; and the barefoot children scrambling round our legs. Here were the black signs charcoaled starkly on the walls: 'Pension La Africana', 'Vinos y Comestibles', 'España Libre', 'Amor! Amor!' Here were the bars and the talking men, the smell of sweet *coñac* and the old dry sherries. A clear cold air, churches and oranges, and a lean-faced generation moving against white walls in sharp silhouettes of scarlet and black. It did not take more than five minutes to wipe out fifteen years and to return me whole to this thorn-cruel, threadbare world, sombre with dead and dying Christs, brassy with glittering Virgins.

We took a room in a hotel which stood close to the harbour's edge, high above the masts of the fishing boats. It was called 'The Queen of the Sea', and its walls were faced with the wave-blue tiles of Seville. Its dining-room was a *patio* of pillars standing under a green-glass roof, and its green furniture was hand-painted with roses, hunting dogs and bulls. The proprietor was a swarthy Moor, morose, fat-necked, with a Farouk-like paunch. He spent his days chewing cold fat pork and playing glum games with the cash register. Ramón, the manager, who was quiet and courtly, had a long face of extreme nobility and torment. The rest of the staff included six chambermaids, four waiters, three kitchen-maids, two washer women, a clerk, a cook, a page-boy, a night-watchman and a turnkey. Yet this hotel was one of the cheapest in the town.

We soon settled in and the place served us well. It was an active, busy inn. The rooms were full of coughs, groans, cries, and laughter; the stairways full of the songs of chamber-maids, and the beds full of fleas—the progenitors of long exhausted dreams. But the food was plentiful. Our first meal, served at half-past two that afternoon, offered us olives, sardines, shell-fish, prawns, a large dish of rice served with meat and saffron, flan and fruit, and a bottle of wine fetched in for a shilling.

After such a meal, drenched in the green, brutish, stimulating oils of the hills, there was nothing one could do. So we climbed to our room overlooking the bay and lay in a lethargy till five o'clock while the girls in the sewing-room above sat singing the langorous songs of their villages.

LAURIE LEE *A Rose For Winter*

4

If thou dost complain, that there shall be a time in the which thou shalt not be, why dost thou not too grieve, that there was a time in the which thou wast not, and so that thou art not as old, as that enlivening planet of time? For, not to have been a thousand years before this moment, is as much to be deplored, as not to be a thousand after it, the effect of them both being one: that will be after us which long long ere we were was. Our children's children have that same reason to murmur that they were not young men in our days, which we now, to complain that we shall not be old in theirs. The violets have their time, though they empurple not the winter, and the roses keep their season, though they discover not their beauty in the spring.

Empires, States, Kingdoms, have by the doom of the Supreme Providence their fatal periods, great cities lie sadly buried in their dust, arts and sciences have not only their eclipses, but their wanings and deaths; the ghastly wonders of the world, raised by the ambition of the ages, are overthrown and trampled; some lights above (deserving to be entitled stars) are loosed and never more seen of us; the excellent fabric of this Universe itself shall one day suffer ruin, or a change like a ruin, and poor Earthlings thus to be handled complain!

WILLIAM DRUMMOND *A Cypresse-Grove*

5

If I should enquire upon what occasion God elected me, and writ my name in the book of Life, I should sooner be afraid that it were not so, than find a reason why it should be so. God made Sun and Moon to distinguish seasons, and day, and night, and we cannot have the fruits of the earth but in their seasons: But God hath made no decree to distinguish the seasons of his mercies; In paradise, the fruits were ripe, the first minute, and in heaven it is always Autumn, his mercies are ever in their maturity. We ask *panem quotidianum*, our daily bread, and God never says you should have come yesterday, he never says you must again tomorrow, but *today if you will hear his voice*, today he will hear you. If some King of the earth have so large an extent of Dominion, in North and South, as that he hath Winter and Summer together in his Dominions, so large an extent East and West, as that he hath day and night together in his Dominions, much more hath God mercy and judgement together: He brought thy Summer out of Winter, though thou have no Spring; though in the ways of fortune or understanding, or conscience, thou have been benighted till now, wintered and frozen, clouded and eclipsed, damped and benumbed, smothered and stupified till now, now God comes to thee, not as in the dawning of the day, not as in the bud of the spring, but as the Sun at noon to illustrate all shadows, as the sheaves in harvest, to fill all penuries, all occasions invite his mercies, and all times are his seasons.

JOHN DONNE Sermons

6

I deny not but that it is of the greatest concernment in the Church and Commonwealth to have a vigilant eye how books demean themselves as well as men; and thereafter to confine, imprison, and do sharpest justice on them as male-factors: for books are not absolutely dead things, but do contain a potency of life in them to be as active as that soul was whose progeny they are; nay, they do preserve as in a vial the purest efficacy and extraction of that living intellect that bred them. I know they are as lively, and as vigorously productive, as those fabulous dragon's teeth; and being sown up and down, may chance to spring up armed men. And yet on the other hand, unless wariness be used, as good almost kill a man as kill a good book; who kills a man kills a reason-able creature, God's image; but he who destroys a good book, kills reason itself, kills the image of God as it were in the eye. Many a man lives a burden to the earth; but a good book is the precious life-blood of a master spirit, embalmed and treasured up on purpose to a life beyond life. 'Tis true, no age can restore a life, whereof perhaps there is no great loss; and revolutions of ages do not oft recover the loss of a rejected truth, for the want of which whole nations fare the worse. We should be wary therefore what persecution we raise against the living labours of public men, how we spill that seasoned life of man preserved and stored up in books; since we see a kind of homicide may be thus committed, sometimes a martyrdom, and if it extend to the whole impression, a kind of massacre, whereof the execution ends not in the slaying of an elemental life, but strikes at that ethereal and fifth essence, the breath of reason itself, slays an immortality rather than a life.

JOHN MILTON Areopagitica

7

We last night received a piece of ill news at our club, which very sensibly afflicted every one of us. I question not but my readers themselves will be troubled at the hearing of it. To keep them no longer in suspense, Sir Roger de Coverley is dead! He departed this life at his house in the country, after a few weeks' sickness. Sir Andrew Freeport has a letter from one of his correspondents in those parts, that informs him the old man caught a cold at the country-sessions as he was very warmly promoting an address of his own penning, in which he succeeded according to his wishes. But this particular comes from a whig justice of the peace, who was always Sir Roger's enemy and antagonist. I have letters both from the chaplain and Captain Sentry, which mention nothing of it, but are filled with many particulars to the honour of the good old man. I have likewise a letter from the butler, who took such good care of me last summer when I was at the knight's house. As my friend the butler mentions, in the simplicity of his heart, several circumstances the others have passed over in silence, I shall give my reader a copy of his letter, without any alteration or diminution.

'Honoured Sir,

'Knowing that you was my old master's good friend, I could not forbear sending you the melancholy news of his death, which has afflicted the whole country, as well as his poor servants, who loved him, I may say, better than we did our lives. I am afraid he caught his death at the last country-sessions, where he would go to see justice done to a poor widow woman, and her fatherless children, that had been wronged by a neighbouring gentleman; for you know, Sir, my good master was always the poor man's friend. Upon his coming home, the first complaint he made was, that he had lost his roast-beef stomach, not being able to touch a sirloin, which was served up according to custom; and you know how he used to take great delight in it. From that time forward he grew worse and worse, but still kept a good heart to the last. Indeed, we were once in great hopes of his recovery, upon a kind message that was sent to him from the widow lady whom he had made love to the forty last years of his life; but this proved only a lightning before death. He has bequeathed to this lady, as a token of his love, a great pearl necklace, and a couple of silver bracelets set with jewels, which belonged to my good old lady his mother. He has bequeathed the fine white gelding that he used to ride a hunting upon to his chaplain, because he thought he would be kind to him; and he has left you all his books. He has, moreover, bequeathed to the chaplain a very pretty tenement with good lands about it. It being a very cold day when he made his will, he left for mourning to every man in the parish a great frieze-coat, and to every woman a black riding-hood. It was a most moving sight to see him take leave of his poor servants, commending us all for our fidelity, whilst we were not able to speak a word for weeping. As we most of us are grown grey-headed in our dear master's service, he has left us pensions and legacies, which we may live very comfortably upon the remaining part of our days. He has bequeathed a great deal more in charity, which is not yet come to my knowledge; and it is peremptorily said in the parish, that he has left money to build a steeple to the church: for he was heard to say some time ago, that, if he lived two years longer, Coverley church should have a steeple to it. The chaplain tells everybody that he made a very good end, and never speaks of him without tears. He was buried, according to his own directions, among the family of the Coverleys, on the left hand of his father Sir Arthur. The coffin was carried by six of his tenants, and the pall held up by six of the quorum. The whole parish followed the corpse with heavy hearts, and in their mourning suits; the men in frieze, and the women in riding-hoods. Captain Sentry, my master's nephew, has taken possession of the Hall-house, and the whole estate. When my old master saw him a little before his death, he shook him by the hand, and wished him joy of the estate which was falling to him, desiring him only to make a good use of it, and to pay the several legacies, and the gifts of charity, which he told him he had left as quit-rents upon the estate. The captain truly seems a courteous man, though he says but little. He makes much of those whom my master loved, and shows great kindness to the old house-dog, that you know my poor master was so fond of. It would have gone to your heart to have heard the moans the dumb creature made on the day of my master's death. He has never enjoyed himself since; no more has any of us. It was the melancholiest day for the poor people that ever happened in Worcestershire. This being all from,

'Honoured Sir, your most sorrowful Servant,

'Edward Biscuit.

'P.S. My master desired, some weeks before he died, that a book, which comes up to you by the carrier, should be given to Sir Andrew Freeport in his name.'

This letter, notwithstanding the poor butler's manner of writing it, gave us such an idea of our good old friend, that upon the reading of it there was not a dry eye in the club. Sir Andrew, opening the book, found it to be a collection of acts of parliament. There was in particular the Act of Uniformity, with some passages in it marked by Sir Roger's own hand. Sir Andrew found that they related to two or three points which he had disputed with Sir Roger, the last time he appeared at the club. Sir Andrew, who would have been merry at such an incident on another occasion, at the sight of the old man's handwriting burst into tears, and put the book into his pocket. Captain Sentry informs me that the knight has left rings and mourning for every one in the club.

JOSEPH ADDISON *The Spectator*

Summarise the argument of the first paragraph:

Lough Ness is about twenty-four miles long, and from one to two miles broad. It is remarkable that Boethius, in his description of Scotland, gives it twelve miles of breadth. When historians or geographers exhibit false accounts of places far distant, they may be forgiven, because they can tell but what they are told; and that their accounts exceed the truth may be justly supposed, because most men exaggerate to others, if not to themselves: but Boethius lived at no great distance; if he never saw the lake, he must have been very incurious, and if he had seen it, his veracity yielded to very slight temptations.

Lough Ness, though not twelve miles broad, is a very remarkable diffusion of water without islands. It fills a large hollow between two ridges of high rocks, being supplied partly by the torrents which fall into it on either side, and partly, as is supposed, by springs at the bottom. Its water is remarkably clear and pleasant, and is imagined by the natives to be medicinal. We were told, that it is in some places a hundred and forty fathom deep, a profundity scarcely credible, and which probably those that relate it have never sounded. Its fish are salmon, trout, and pike.

It was said at Fort Augustus, that Lough Ness is open in the hardest winters, though a lake not far from it is covered with ice. In discussing these exceptions from the course of nature, the first question is, whether the fact be justly stated. That which is strange is delightful, and a pleasing error is not willingly detected. Accuracy of narration is not very common, and there are few so rigidly philosophical, as not to represent as perpetual, what is only frequent, or as constant, what is really casual. If it be true that Lough Ness never freezes, it is either sheltered by its high banks from the cold blasts, and exposed only to those winds which have more power to agitate than congeal; or it is kept in perpetual motion by the rush of streams from the rocks that enclose it. Its profundity though it should be such as is represented can have little part in this exemption; for though deep wells are not frozen, because their water is secluded from the external air, yet where a wide surface is exposed to the full influence of a freezing atmosphere, I know not why the depth should keep it open. Natural philosophy is now one of the favourite studies of the Scottish nation, and Lough Ness well deserves to be diligently examined.

SAMUEL JOHNSON *Journey to the Western Isles of Scotland*

9

It is now sixteen or seventeen years since I saw the queen of France, then the dauphiness, at Versailles; and surely never lighted on this orb, which she hardly seemed to touch, a more delightful vision. I saw her just above the horizon, decorating and cheering the elevated sphere she just began to move in; glittering like the morning star, full of life, and splendour, and joy. Oh! what a revolution! and what an heart must I have to contemplate without emotion that elevation and that fall! Little did I dream when she added titles of veneration to those of enthusiastic, distant, respectful love, that she should ever be obliged to carry the sharp antidote against disgrace concealed in that bosom; little did I dream that I should have lived to see such disasters fallen upon her in a nation of gallant men, in a nation of men of honour and of cavaliers. I thought ten thousand swords must have leaped from their scabbards to avenge even a look that threatened her with insult. – But the age of chivalry is gone. That of sophisters, economists, and calculators has succeeded; and the glory of Europe is extinguished for ever. Never, never more, shall we behold that generous loyalty to rank and sex, that proud submission, that dignified obedience, that subordination of the heart, which kept alive, even in servitude itself, the spirit of an exalted freedom. The unbought grace of life, the cheap defence of nations, the nurse of manly sentiment and heroic enterprise is gone! It is gone, that sensibility of principle, that chastity of honour, which felt a stain like a wound, which inspired courage whilst it mitigated ferocity, which ennobled whatever it touched, and under which vice itself lost half its evil, by losing all its grossness.

EDMUND BURKE *Reflections on the Revolution in France*

10

The elders, with whom I was brought up, were of a character not likely to let slip the sacred observance of any old institution; and the ringing out of the Old Year was kept by them with circumstances of peculiar ceremony. In those days the sound of those midnight chimes, though it seemed to raise hilarity in all around me, never failed to bring a train of pensive imagery into my fancy. Yet I then scarce conceived what it meant, or thought of it as a reckoning that concerned me. Not childhood alone, but the young man till thirty, never feels practically that he is mortal. He knows it indeed, and, if need were, he could preach a homily on the fragility of life; but he brings it not home to himself, any more than in a hot June we can appropriate to our imagination the freezing days of December. But now, shall I confess a truth?—I feel these audits but too powerfully. I begin to count the probabilities of my duration, and to grudge at the expenditure of moments and shortest periods, like misers' farthings. In proportion as the years both lessen and shorten, I set more count upon their periods, and would fain lay my ineffectual finger upon the spoke of the great wheel. I am not content to pass away 'like a weaver's shuttle'. Those metaphors solace me not, nor sweeten the unpalatable draught of mortality. I care not to be carried with the tide, that smoothly bears human life to eternity; and reluct at the inevitable course of destiny. I am in love with this green earth; the face of town and country; the unspeakable rural solitudes, and the sweet security of streets. I would set up my tabernacle here. I am content to stand still at the age to which I am arrived; I, and my friends: to be no younger, no richer, no handsomer. I do not want to be weaned by age; or drop, like mellow fruit, as they say, into the grave. Any alteration, on this earth of mine, in diet or in lodging, puzzles and discomposes me. My household-gods plant a terrible fixed foot, and are not rooted up without blood. They do not willingly seek Lavinian shores. A new state of being staggers me.

11

Briefly summarise the argument of the passage.

A poet in our times is a semi-barbarian in a civilised community. He lives in the days that are past. His ideas, thoughts, feelings, associations, are all with barbarous manners, obsolete customs, and exploded superstitions. The march of his intellect is like that of a crab, backward. The brighter the light diffused around him by the progress of reason, the thicker is the darkness of antiquated barbarism, in which he buries himself like a mole, to throw up the barren hillocks of his Cimmerian labours. The philosophic mental tranquillity which looks round with an equal eye on all external things, collects a store of ideas, discriminates their relative value, assigns to all their proper place, and from the materials of useful knowledge thus collected, appreciated, and arranged, forms new combinations that impress the stamp of their power and utility on the real business of life, is diametrically the reverse of that frame of mind which poetry inspires, or from which poetry can emanate. The highest inspirations of poetry are resolvable into three ingredients: the rant of un-regulated passion, the whining of exaggerated feeling, and the cant of factitious sentiment: and can therefore serve only to ripen a splendid lunatic like Alexander, a puling driveller like Werter, or a morbid dreamer like Wordsworth. It can never make a philosopher, nor a statesman, nor in any class of life an useful or rational man. It cannot claim the slightest share in any one of the comforts and utilities of life of which we have witnessed so many and so rapid advances. But though not useful, it may be said it is highly ornamental, and deserves to be cultivated for the pleasure it yields. Even if this be granted, it does not follow that a writer of poetry in the present state of society is not a waster of his own time, and a robber of that of others. Poetry is not one of those arts which, like painting, require repetition and multiplication, in order to be diffused among society. There are more good poems already existing than are sufficient to employ that portion of life which any mere reader and recipient of poetical impressions should devote to them, and these having been produced in poetical times, are far superior in all the characteristics of poetry to the artificial reconstructions of a few morbid ascetics in unpoetical times. To read the promiscuous rubbish of the present time to the exclusion of the select treasures of the past, is to substitute the worse for the better variety of the same mode of enjoyment.

THOMAS LOVE PEACOCK *The Four Ages of Poetry*

12

Briefly summarise the argument.

Like other tyrannies, the tyranny of the majority was at first, and is still vulgarly, held in dread, chiefly as operating through the acts of the public authorities. But reflecting persons perceived that when society is itself the tyrant—society collectively over the separate individuals who compose it—its means of tyrannising are not restricted to the acts which it may do by the hands of its political functionaries. Society can and does execute its own mandates: and if it issues wrong mandates instead of right, or any mandates at all in things with which it ought not to meddle, it practises a social tyranny more formidable than many kinds of political oppression, since, though not usually upheld by such extreme penalties, it leaves fewer means of escape, penetrating much more deeply into the details of life, and enslaving the soul itself. Protection, therefore, against the tyranny of the magistrate is not enough: there needs protection also against the tyranny of the prevailing opinion and feeling; against the tendency of society to impose, by other means than civil penalties, its own ideas and practices as rules of conduct on those who dissent from them; to fetter the development, and, if possible, prevent the formation, of any individuality not in harmony with its ways, and compel all characters to fashion themselves upon the model of its own. There is a limit to the legitimate inferference of collective opinion with individual independence: and to find that limit, and maintain it against encroachment, is as indispensable to a good conduct of human affairs, as protection against political despotism.

JOHN STUART MILL On Liberty

13

At the conclusion of dinner, a maid entered the room with a white cashmere mantle, placing it over the shoulders of her young lady, as she said the carriage was waiting.

Lady Isabel advanced to the earl. 'Goodbye, papa.'

'Good night, my love,' he answered, drawing her to him, and kissing her sweet face. 'Tell Mrs Vane I will not have you kept out till morning hours: you are but a child yet. Mr Carlyle, will you ring? I am debarred from seeing my daughter to the carriage.'

'If your lordship will allow me – if Lady Isabel will pardon the attendance of one little used to wait upon young ladies, I shall be proud to see her to her carriage,' was the somewhat confused answer of Mr Carlyle, as he touched the bell.

The earl thanked him, the young lady smiled, and Mr Carlyle conducted her down the broad, lighted staircase, and stood bareheaded by the door of the luxurious chariot, and handed her in. She put out her hand in her frank, pleasant manner, as she wished him good-night. The carriage rolled on its way, and Mr Carlyle returned to the earl.

'Well, is she not a handsome girl?' he demanded.

'Handsome is not the word for beauty such as hers,' was

Mr Carlyle's reply, in a low, warm tone, 'I never saw a face half so beautiful.'

'She caused quite a sensation at the Drawing-room last week – as I hear. This everlasting gout kept me indoors all day. And she is as good as she is beautiful.'

The earl was not partial. Lady Isabel was wondrously gifted by nature, not only in mind and person, but in heart. She was as little like a fashionable young lady as it was well possible to be, partly because she had hitherto been secluded from the great world, partly from the care bestowed upon her training. During the lifetime of her mother, she had lived occasionally at East Lynne, but mostly at a larger seat of the earl's in Wales, Mount Severn: since her mother's death, she had remained entirely at Mount Severn, under the charge of a judicious governess, a very small establishment being kept up for them, and the earl paying them impromptu and flying visits. Generous and benevolent she was; timid and sensitive to a degree; gentle and considerate to all. Do not cavil at her being thus praised: admire and love her while you may, she is worthy of it now, in her innocent girlhood: the time will come when such praise would be misplaced. Could the fate that was to overtake his child have been foreseen by the earl, he would have struck her down to death, in his love, as she stood before him, rather than suffer her to enter upon it.

14

Lastly – take the Art of Building – the strongest – proudest – most orderly – most enduring of the arts of man; that of which the produce is in the surest manner accumulative, and need not perish, or be replaced; but if once well done, will stand more strongly than the unbalanced rocks – more prevalently than the crumbling hills. The art which is associated with all civil pride and sacred principle; with which men record their power – satisfy their enthusiasm – make sure their defence – define and make dear their habitation. And in six thousand years of building, what have we done? Of the greater part of all that skill and strength, *no* vestige is left, but fallen stones, that encumber the fields and impede the streams. But, from this waste of disorder, and of time, and of rage, what *is* left to us? Constructive and progressive creatures, that we are, with ruling brains, and forming hands, capable of fellowship, and thirsting for fame, can we not contend, in comfort, with the insects of the forest, or, in achievement, with the worm of the sea? The white surf rages in vain against the ramparts built by poor atoms of scarcely nascent life; but only ridges of formless ruin mark the places where once dwelt our noblest multitudes. The ant and the moth have cells for each of their young, but our little ones lie in festering heaps, in homes that consume them like graves; and night by night, from the corners of our streets, rises up the cry of the homeless – 'I was a stranger, and ye took me not in.'

JOHN RUSKIN Sesame and Lilies

15

What I have most wanted to do throughout the past ten years is to make political writing into an art. My starting point is always a feeling of partisanship, a sense of injustice. When I sit down to write a book, I do not say to myself, 'I am going to produce a work of art.' I write it because there is some lie that I want to expose, some fact to which I want to draw attention, and my initial concern is to get a hearing. But I could not do the work of writing a book, or even a long magazine article, if it were not also an aesthetic experience. Anyone who cares to examine my work will see that even when it is downright propaganda it contains much that a full-time politician would consider irrelevant. I am not able, and I do not want, completely to abandon the world-view that I acquired in childhood. So long as I remain alive and well I shall continue to feel strongly about prose style, to love the surface of the earth, and to take pleasure in solid objects and scraps of useless information. It is no use trying to suppress that side of myself. The job is to reconcile my ingrained likes and dislikes with the essentially public, non-individual activities that this age forces on all of us.

It is not easy. It raises problems of construction and of language, and it raises in a new way the problem of truthfulness. Let me give just one example of the cruder kind of difficulty that arises. My book about the Spanish Civil War, *Homage to Catalonia*, is, of course, a frankly political book, but in the main it is written with a certain detachment and regard for form. I did try very hard in it to tell the whole truth without violating my literary instincts. But among other things it contains a long chapter full of newspaper quotations and the like, defending the Trotskyists who were accused of plotting with Franco. Clearly such a chapter, which after a year or two would lose its interest for any ordinary reader, must ruin the book. A critic whom I respect read me a lecture about it. 'Why did you put in all that stuff?' he said. 'You've turned what might have been a good book into journalism.' I happened to know, what very few people in England had been allowed to know, that innocent men were being falsely accused. If I had not been angry about that I should never have written the book.

In one form or another this problem comes up again. The problem of language is subtler and would take too long to discuss. I will only say that of late years I have tried to write less picturesquely and more exactly. In any case I find that by the time you have perfected any style of writing, you have always outgrown it. *Animal Farm* was the first book in which I tried, with full consciousness of what I was doing, to fuse political purpose and artistic purpose into one whole. I have not written a novel for seven years, but I hope to write another fairly soon. It is bound to be a failure, every book is a failure, but I do know with some clarity what kind of book I want to write.

Looking back through the last page or two, I see that I have made it appear as though my motives in writing were wholly public-spirited. I don't want to leave that as the final impression. All writers are vain, selfish, and lazy, and at the very bottom of their motives there lies a mystery. Writing a book is a horrible, exhausting struggle, like a long bout of some painful illness. One would never undertake such a thing if one were not driven on by some demon whom one can neither resist nor understand. For all one knows that demon is simply the same instinct that makes a baby squall for attention. And yet it is also true that one can write nothing readable unless one constantly struggles to efface one's own personality. Good prose is like a window pane. I cannot say with certainty which of my motives are the strongest, but I know which of them deserve to be followed. And looking back through my work, I see that it is invariably where I lacked a *political* purpose that I wrote lifeless books and was betrayed into purple passages, sentences without meaning, decorative adjectives and humbug generally.

GEORGE ORWELL *Why I Write* [from *Such, Such Were the Joys*]

Modern prose for critical practice

1

This passage is the beginning of *Riders in the Chariot* by Patrick White. What qualities in the novel as a whole does this opening lead you to expect? Indicate the aspects of content and style in the extract that appear to justify your answer.

'Who was that woman?' asked Mrs Colquhoun, a rich lady who had come recently to live at Sarsaparilla.

'Ah,' Mrs Sugden said, and laughed, 'that was Miss Hare.'

'She appears an unusual sort of person,' Mrs Colquhoun ventured to hope.

'Well,' replied Mrs Sugden, 'I cannot deny that Miss Hare is *different*.'

But the postmistress would not add to that. She started poking at a dry sponge. Even at her most communicative, talking with authority of the weather, which was her subject, she favoured the objective approach.

Mrs Colquhoun was able to see for herself that Miss Hare was a small, freckled thing, whose stockings, at that moment, could have been coming down. To tell the truth, Mrs Colquhoun was somewhat put out by the postmistress's discretion, but could not remain so indefinitely, for the War was over, and the peace had not yet set hard.

Miss Hare continued to walk away from the post office, through the smell of moist nettle, under the pale disc of the sun. An early pearliness of light, a lamb's-wool of morning promised the millenium, yet, between the road and the shed in which the Godbolds lived, the burnt-out blackberry bushes, lolling and waiting in rusty coils, suggested that the enemy might not have withdrawn. As Miss Hare passed, several barbs of several strands attached themselves to the folds of her skirt, pulling on it, tight, tighter, until she was all spread out behind, part woman, part umbrella.

'You could get torn,' Mrs Godbold warned, who had come up to the edge of the road, in search of something, whether child, goat, or perhaps just the daily paper.

'Oh, I could get torn,' Miss Hare answered. 'But what is a little tear?'

It did not matter.

Mrs Godbold was rather large. She smiled at the ground, incredulous, but glad.

'I saw a wombat,' Miss Hare called.

'Not a wombat! In these parts? I do not believe you!' Mrs Godbold answered back

Miss Hare laughed.

'What did it look like?' Mrs Godbold called, and laughed. Still looking in the grass.

'I will tell you,' Miss Hare declared, laughing, but always walking away.

It did not matter to either that much would remain un-explained. It did not matter that neither had looked at the other's face, for each was aware that the moment could yield no more than they already knew. Somewhere in the past, that particular relationship had been fully ratified.

2

What aims do you think the writer of this autobiographical passage had? Discuss the methods used to convey his recollections of the past and to establish his attitude to them.

In October 1904, I sailed from Tilbury Docks in the P & O *Syria* for Ceylon. I was a Cadet in the Ceylon Civil Service. To make a complete break with one's former life is a strange, frightening, and exhilarating experience. It has upon one, I think, the effect of a second birth. When one emerges from one's mother's womb one leaves a life of dim security for a world of violent difficulties and dangers. Few, if any, people ever entirely recover from the trauma of being born, and we spend a lifetime unsuccessfully trying to heal the wound, to protect ourselves against the hostility of things and men. But because at birth consciousness is dim and it takes a long time for us to become aware of our environment, we do not feel a sudden break, and adjustment is slow, lasting indeed a lifetime. I can remember the precise moment of my second birth. The umbilical cord by which I had been attached to my family, to St Paul's, to Cambridge and Trinity was cut when, leaning over the ship's taffrail, I watched through the dirty, dripping murk and fog of the river my mother and sister waving good-bye and felt the ship begin slowly to move down the Thames to the sea.

LEONARD WOOLF *Growing*

3

Write a criticism of this passage.

There aren't many people in the tea-garden now, only an old couple and a young couple sitting at opposite tables. The old couple sit very still, immobilised in contentment. The man has a stiff blue suit and a gold watch-chain festooned with little badges across his waistcoat; his thick-soled brown boots glitter with polish, and his bowler, set firmly on his head, is as dignified as a cardinal's hat. Even the white cricket-shirt, open at the neck and spread out Byronically over his jacket, cannot destroy this dignity, the strange indestructible quality which comes unasked and unawares at the end of a lifetime's hard and ill-paid work. His wife, mountainous in flowered cretonne and a red hat with a green feather, sits with her hands folded in her lap, a look of quiet enjoyment on her face. They have about them a humbleness which makes one almost angry; they look as if they were frightened someone would take the evening away from them.

The young couple are an exact definition of what Wilfred

137

Pickles means by Courting. The boy wears the summer best of the working-classes—a check jacket with plain flannels of the same colour, and thick-soled brogues—a fashion ten years out of date and worn with a morning-coat stiffness instead of casually. His girl with her neat, mousy hair and make-up applied with such odd, frightened discreetness that it makes her look ten years older than she really is, wears a pink rayon dress and a beige coat, both in those strange Blackersford shades which never show the dirt but never look clean. She's that most respectable of institutions, the Young Lady who is about to become a Fiancée. And her young man, though he can't be more than twenty, has already settled down: one can see at a glance that when they're married they'll call each other Mother and Father. But not yet; tonight they're not respectable, they hold hands shamelessly and look into each other's eyes; the dark is waiting for them.

The old couple don't stare at them, they don't speak to them, yet one can sense an infinite indulgence, an almost pagan approval. The young couple suddenly rise and leave the tea-garden, their arms round each other's waists. 'Ah knaw wheer they're going,' the old man says, and laughs comfortably. 'Number Nine Rock,' says his wife. They nod like mandarins and the old woman's huge bosom jiggles with amusement. 'Too late for us nah, Josh,' she says. 'Nay, doan't say that, lass,' he says, and squeezes her waist. 'Well, Ah nivver. Thar't a fond'un,' she says tenderly, and he assumes a doggish air.

JOHN BRAINE *Number Nine Rock* [from the *New Statesman*]

4

Describe the writer's attitude (*a*) to the televised Coronation scene; and (*b*) to his fellow-watchers. What is their attitude to the Coronation?

The Trust hotel had been careful to provide television, so that Coronation day passed for us as it did for most others.

Perhaps if I had viewed the ceremony in my home, I should have been able to preserve my scepticism, my innate Republicanism. Soothed by the familiarity of my own surroundings, the comments of my own small world, I should have sunk easily into my comfortable prejudices. As it was, I sat in a draught, surrounded by the uneasy comments of the saloon bar gang. Never have I seen Good-Scoutery less at ease; they had come with that Rotarian, have-the-next-one-on-me-old-boy jollity that they had found so infallible at a thousand business dinners, Legion reunions and family gatherings. It was a big, British occasion, and no people, of course, were more British than they. It was fascinating to see them fight the strange beauty, the formal Byzantinism of the ceremony that appeared upon the screen. They were prepared, of course, for an occasional catch in the throat, a moment of lowered head, but the elaborate grace before them demanded less perfunctory reverence. There is no English *milieu* less sympathetic than that of the Frothblowers' Anthem; it was nice to see the 'gang' so put out when they least expected it.

ANGUS WILSON *Throughout the country* [from the *New Statesman*]

5

Identify the linguistic features that signal tone and intention in this passage.

'We're going through!' The Commander's voice was like thin ice breaking. He wore his full-dress uniform, with the heavily braided white cap pulled down rakishly over one cold grey eye. 'We can't make it, sir. It's spoiling for a hurricane, if you ask me.' 'I'm not asking you, Lieutenant Berg,' said the Commander. 'Throw on the power lights! Rev her up to 8,500! We're going through!' The pounding of the cylinders increased: ta-pocketa-pocketa-pocketa-*pocketa-pocketa*. The Commander stared at the ice forming on the pilot window. He walked over and twisted a row of complicated dials. 'Switch on No. 8 auxiliary!' he shouted.

'Switch on No. 8 auxiliary!' repeated Lieutenant Berg. 'Full strength in No. 3 turret!' shouted the Commander. 'Full strength in No. 3 turret!' The crew, bending to their various tasks in the huge, hurtling eight-engined Navy hydroplane, looked at each other and grinned. 'The Old Man'll get us through,' they said to one another. 'The Old Man ain't afraid of Hell!' . . .

'Not so fast! You're driving too fast!' said Mrs Mitty. 'What are you driving so fast for?'

'Hmm?' said Walter Mitty. He looked at his wife, in the seat beside him, with shocked astonishment. She seemed grossly unfamiliar, like a strange woman who had yelled at him in a crowd. 'You were up to fifty-five,' she said. 'You know I don't like to go more than forty. You were up to fifty-five.' Walter Mitty drove on towards Waterbury in silence, the roaring of the SN202 through the worst storm in twenty years of Navy flying fading in the remote, intimate airways of his mind. 'You're tensed up again,' said Mrs Mitty. 'It's one of your days. I wish you'd let Dr Renshaw look you over.'

JAMES THURBER *The Secret Life of Walter Mitty*
[from *My World and Welcome To It*]

6

Briefly summarise the argument of the following passage; identify the kind of writing; and estimate the author's success in carrying out his intentions.

We have not yet adapted ourselves to the implications of the fact that women now have two roles to play, the one as demanding and as respectable as the other. The idea that a married woman need not work can now be seen as a short-lived middle-class reaction to the Industrial Revolution, which took work out of the home and consigned it to the factory. The Curlylocks ideal of the conspicuously leisured middle-class wife is outdated to the point where most women are liable to feel guilt or lack of fulfilment if they have no form of outside activity. (Ninety per cent of Mrs Gavron's sample proposed to go back to work when their children were older.) This means that a more conscious effort must be made to provide the training and education for the middle-aged woman that will help her to rise above the unskilled level of employment to which she is often confined. Many employers still do not realise that married women workers are no temporary aberration but are here to stay. Adjustment seems to be most easily made in those areas, like Lancashire, where the tradition of married women's work is longest established. But for the most part the structure of industry and the professions is ill-designed to meet the special circumstances of married women. This is not just a matter of providing more scope for part-time work or shopping breaks. In justice both to society and to the women themselves it will have to be ensured that the rise to positions of responsibility is not unduly prejudiced by the discontinuity occasioned by child-bearing.

Equally pressing is the need to extend more recognition to the position of the housewife. Of the two social categories most vulnerable to mental illness, one is the older woman whose children have grown up, and who feels useless because she has nothing to do. The other is the young mother, cooped up in her flat with small children, isolated from the community, and occupied in an unbroken routine of drudgery, which is not only arduous but is positively despised by the rest of society as not 'real work'. We must, as Mrs Gavron says, be brought to recognise the multiplicity of roles which women have to perform. Educational systems too often present girls with a desperately misleading choice between marriage and a career. This alternative caused much heart-searching in the past: it need no longer exist, for the two vocations can be combined. But before such a combination can be achieved at every social level, without tension and unhappiness, many sharp adjustments will have to be made. Some of these are practical matters of economic organisation but others involve a more subtle change of attitude and unspoken assumptions. To reshape opinion is a harder business than merely changing the letter of the law. But such changes will have to be accomplished if it is to cease to be a disadvantage to have been born a woman.

KEITH THOMAS *The Captive Wife* [from the *New Statesman*]

7

Outline the contrasts made here between Bridges and Kipling. What conclusions can be drawn from this passage about the writer's views on poetry?

But though Bridges was in no sense a 'modernist' poet, he reflects one of the predicaments that have created modern poetry. One of the reasons why it is impossible to agree with Yvor Winter in assigning major status to Bridges is that his voice seems so remote from the urgent and harsh voices of common speech in his time. The high and fine traditional tone seems to impinge nowhere on everyday life. It is thin and distant even where Bridges is lamenting the failure of the poets in the 1890s to bring a trumpet-voice to public affairs.

> Lament, fair hearted queen, lament with me . . .
> For when thy seer died no song was sung
> Nor for our heroes fal'n by land and sea
>   Hath honour found a tongue.

The lines have a very cool, formal, distant ring; and when Bridges himself became Poet Laureate he steadfastly eschewed the poem on the public occasion, leaving honour to find, for our heroes fallen by land or sea, the more urgent and brassy tongue of Rudyard Kipling. Kipling's special kind of success and failure showed that, in the late Victorian and Edwardian ages, it was becoming more and more difficult to strike a common note without catching a 'common' tone. As T. S. Eliot has said in a fine essay, Kipling is not setting out to write 'poetry' in the ordinary sense at all. What is remarkable is that the hymn and ballad metres, the frank intentions of journalistic propaganda or amusement, the drum-thumpings, the

Cockney impersonations, so often fail to prevent Kipling from writing poetry. George Orwell has at once praised and condemned him as the poet of the copy-book headings, the memorable platitudes which stick in the mind often because, in a nasty and nagging way, they are uncomfortably true. From an opposite political point of view, both Orwell and Eliot see Kipling as the poet of Imperial responsibility. Kipling first caught the public ear with a poetry of popular impersonation: trying to imitate the talk of Cockneys and tramps, the soldier and the uneducated man. In this sense Kipling is a 'modern' writer in a way in which Bridges is not: his complexity took the form of a too artful imitation of simplicity, but he did manage for a time to bridge the growing gap between poetry and the public, although he often paid too high a price.

G. S. FRASER *The Modern Writer and His World*

8

Summarise briefly the argument of this passage and add your own comments on it. Discuss the effectiveness of the style.

But it may be useful to discuss what we mean by Art a little further. The air is full of sentimentalities and false notions about it, and should be cleared. A good many people – especially democratic people – will say the question of Art and Artists has already been answered, and point to William Morris and the Arts and Crafts. This is very dangerous . . . Morris said, I believe, that all poetry ought to be of the kind a man can make up while he is working at a loom. Much of his own was. That may be why a lot of it is so dull. 'Easy writing,' someone said, 'makes damned hard reading.' Not so did Shakespeare or Balzac write or Beethoven compose. It is an infamous heresy of his, and it extends to other arts besides poetry, though it is about poetry most people hold it. It leads to this too common idea that the various artists of the future will be able to do ordinary work for so many hours a day, and pursue their arts in their leisure time. You don't find artists advocating that: only some of the ordinary cultured public. It is a thing we can't allow. It means the death of the Arts, a civilisation of amiable amateurs, of inter-mittent Alexandrians. We have too much of this system already—it is no fault of the individual—the Civil Service poets, the stockbroker who does water-colours in the evenings, the music-master who has the holidays to compose in. Better almost, a literature of blue-books than a literature of belles-lettres.

There is another wrong notion of art that falsifies the opinions of many on this subject. Let us beware of those who talk of 'the art of the people', or of 'expressing the soul of the Community'. The Community hasn't got a soul; you can't voice the soul of the Community any more than you can blow its nose. The conditions of Democracy may profoundly alter the outlook of many artists, and partly their style and subject matter. But the *main* business of art has been, is, and, one must assume, will be an individual and unique affair. 'I saw—*I* saw,' the artist says, 'a tree against the sky, or a blank wall in the sunlight, and it was so thrilling, so arresting, so particularly itself, that—well really, I *must* show you . . . There!' Or the writer explains, 'Just so and just so it happened, or might happen, and thus the heart shook, and thus . . .' And suddenly, deliciously, with them you see and feel.

Art is not a criticism of Life. There *is* a side of it that makes problems clear, throws light on the complexity of modern life, assists one to understand. It is a function much dwelt on nowadays. A section of modern drama is praised for explain-ing religion, or the relation of the sexes, or of Capital and Labour. It is incidental. Discussion is merely one of the means, not the end, of literary art. You are in the midst of insoluble problems of temperance reform and education and organisa-tion. The artist, as artist, is not concerned. He leads you away by the hand and, Mamillius-like, begins his tale: 'There was a man—dwelt by a churchyard'—it is purely irrelevant.

RUPERT BROOKE *Democracy and the Arts*